USS North Carolina

Written by David Doyle

Squadron at Sea

Squadron Signal Publications

Cover Art by Don Greer

Line Illustrations by Todd Sturgell

(Front Cover) The crew of *North Carolina* conducts gunnery trials following repairs and modernization at Pearl Harbor in November 1942.

(Back Cover) *North Carolina,* wearing a dazzle camouflage scheme, designated Measure 32/18D, patrols the Pacific in November 1944.

About the Squadron At Sea Series

The *Squadron At Sea* series details a specific ship using color and black-and-white archival photographs and photographs of in-service, preserved, and restored equipment. *Squadron At Sea* titles are devoted to civilian and military vessels, while *On Deck®* titles are devoted to warships. These picture books focus on specific vessels from the laying of the keel to present or its finale.

 Proudly printed in the U.S.A.
Copyright 2011 Squadron/Signal Publications
1115 Crowley Drive, Carrollton, TX 75006-1312 U.S.A.

Hard Cover ISBN 978-0-89747-648-5
Soft Cover ISBN 978-0-89747-647-8

Military/Combat Photographs and Snapshots

If you have any photos of aircraft, armor, soldiers, or ships of any nation, particularly wartime snapshots, please share them with us and help make Squadron/Signal's books all the more interesting and complete in the future. Any photograph sent to us will be copied and returned. Electronic images are preferred. The donor will be fully credited for any photos used. Please send them to:

Squadron/Signal Publications
1115 Crowley Drive
Carrollton, TX 75006-1312 U.S.A.
www.SquadronSignalPublications.com

(Title Page) The clean teak decks of *North Carolina,* spotless here during her August 1941 military trials, would soon give way to guns and camouflage paint as she fought her way through every major battle in the Pacific.

Acknowledgments

The preparation of this book was a substantial undertaking, and the completion of this project required the help of many individuals, some of whom have devoted years to researching the *North Carolina.* Their unselfish help is deeply appreciated In particular I would like to thank Tom Kailbourn; Tracy White (Researcher at Large); Ron Smith; Scott Taylor; Robert Hanshew with the Navy History and Heritage Command; Kim Sincox and Mary Ames Booker at the Battleship *North Carolina;* Hampton Roads Naval Museum; Cristy Gallardo and Lance Skidmore at Puget Sound Naval Shipyard; the Naval Historical Foundation; and Stan Piet. The dedicated and talented staff at Squadron Publications capably assembled this volume, and painstakingly restored aging, damaged photos. My darling wife Denise scanned the vast majority of the photos on these pages, in addition to providing unflagging encouragement and support during long hours of research.

Introduction

When the USS *North Carolina* (BB-55) was launched in 1940, she was a much-needed source of pride for a nation staggering in the throes of a depression and worried by winds of war sweeping across Europe and the East Asia. Soon after her fitting out, the *North Carolina,* her men, and the nation found themselves swept up in the global conflict that was WWII. *North Carolina's* men earned themselves a reputation of competence and camaraderie as they fought their way through every major naval offensive in the Pacific Theater. *North Carolina* earned 12 battle stars, symbolic of her participation in these campaigns, becoming the most decorated U.S. battleship of the war. These honors were not without cost, with 10 men killed in action aboard the ship, another six from non-combat causes, and 64 men wounded.

The trip from the drawing board to the waters of New York's Wallabout Bay, though less dangerous, was fraught with hazards of its own. *North Carolina* was built under the guidelines of the Second London Naval Treaty, which imposed strict limits on weight and armament. When Congress authorized her construction on 3 June 1936, it had been 16 years since the United States had built a new battleship. A series of three treaties (the Washington as well as the First and Second London Treaties) along with changing demands by the U.S. Navy General Board kept designers scrambling. As construction was begun it was intended that she mount 12 14-inch guns in three triple turrets – a last-minute change to the new 16-inch, 45-caliber weapons caused weeks of delay as plans were altered and material orders updated. Just as she threaded her way through the bureaucracy of that age, weathered the hazards of the enemy as well as a typhoon, she skirted the scrapper's torch. Today she is preserved as a memorial in Wilmington, North Carolina – an enduring symbol of pride for a nation grateful for the service of her crew, and the skill of the tradesmen who crafted her.

Several U.S. Navy ships with the name North Carolina preceded BB-55, the subject of this book, first of which was a ship of the line launched in 1820. The second *North Carolina,* designated Armored Cruiser 12, was launched in 1906. That ship is seen here during World War I, exhibiting her dazzle camouflage pattern. (Battleship *North Carolina*)

Work on Battleship 52, which was earmarked to be named the *North Carolina,* began at Norfolk Navy Yard in January 1919 but was discontinued on 8 February 1922 pursuant to the limitations of the Washington Naval Treaty. The uncompleted ship was sold for scrap metal in October 1923. The ship would have been 684 feet long, displacing 43,200 tons. (National Archives)

Immediately preceding the USS *North Carolina* (BB-55) in construction was the USS *West Virginia* (BB-48). Commissioned on 1 December 1923, she embodied many improvements over battleships built before World War I, including watertight compartmentalization of the hull and enhanced armor protection. (National Archives)

On 23 June 1937, members of the Construction and Repair Division, Department of the Navy, work on plans for two new battleships: the USS *North Carolina* (BB-55) and USS *Washington* (BB-56). Numerous designs were proposed for this class of ships before the final ones were approved, and masses of blueprints were produced before the keels were laid. (Library of Congress)

Officials gather around a sign commemorating the keel-laying ceremony for the *North Carolina*. It had been 15 years since a U.S. battleship had been commissioned, and the country was slowly making its way out of the Great Depression. Hence, the construction of the *North Carolina* was an important event in the economic and military life of that era. (Battleship *North Carolina*)

An overhead view shows the size of the crowd attending the 27 October 1937 laying of the keel for the *North Carolina* at Building Ways No. 2, U.S. Navy Yard, New York, also known as the Brooklyn Navy Yard. Civilians made up most of the crowd. At the center of the photo, a riveting machine dangles from a hoist above the first two keel sections to be joined together. (National Archives)

A crouching workman with a white cap positions a rivet on a keel section, while an officer to the left and a man wearing a fedora to the right guide a suspended riveting machine into place. The riveting machine is hanging from a chain fall. The section of keel riveted that day was 70 feet long. Building materials are piled up on the building way in the background. (National Archives)

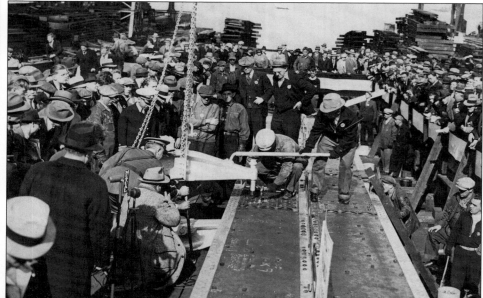

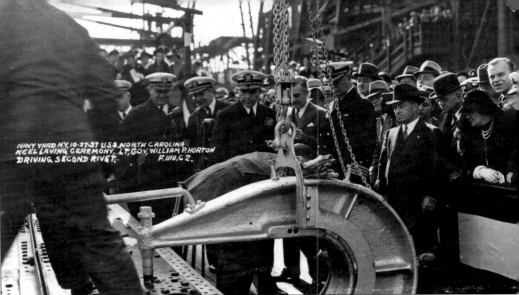

Vice Admiral Clark H. Woodward, commandant of the Navy Yard, New York, and two civilian dignitaries, possibly Assistant Secretary of the Navy Charles Edison (left) and Lt. Gov. Wilkins P. Horton of North Carolina (right), watch approvingly as a rivet is driven into the keel. Those three men drove the first three rivets in the keel of the *North Carolina*. (National Archives)

Vice Admiral Clark H. Woodward prepares to shoot the third rivet into the keel of the *North Carolina* on 27 October 1937. Assistant Secretary of the Navy Charles Edison, son of inventor Thomas Edison, had driven the first rivet into the keel. According to press reports, before the crowd left the ceremony, professional riveters had moved in and were hard at work. (National Archives)

North Carolina's lieutenant governor, Wilkins P. Horton (who is incorrectly identified as "William" in the original caption), drives the second rivet into the keel of the *North Carolina*. He is only partially visible behind the suspended riveting machine. Standing next to him is Vice Admiral Woodward. (National Archives)

On 5 April 1938, the status of work amidships on *North Carolina* is viewed from the port side looking aft, showing the shell (outer plating of the hull) and keel (fore and aft girder) under construction. The ship would have a triple-bottom structure to protect against underwater detonations, incorporating a lower tier with oil bunkers and water tanks and an upper tier of void compartments. The placement of voids and tanks was specially engineered to absorb combat damage, protecting vital areas. (National Archives)

NAVY YARD NY 10-3-38. NORTH CAROLINA
VIEW LOOKING AFT FROM BHD 31
FMB-514

An overhead view of work on *North Carolina* dated 20 June 1938 was taken from amidships facing aft. As the hull is constructed, lateral frames will be extended outward from the center; longitudinal frames will be built, fore to aft; and the frames will be fastened to the shell. Scaffolding erected along the building ways will be used in constructing the sides of the hull. (National Archives)

From a vantage point similar to that in the preceding photo, construction on the *North Carolina* is viewed facing aft on 3 October 1938. In the foreground is a transverse bulkhead, flanked by frames for the longitudinal bulkheads. The steel plating on the transverse bulkhead has been installed. Later, machinery would go into the space at the bottom of the photo. (National Archives)

This overhead photo of construction on the *North Carolina* incorporates the area from Bulkhead 84 forward to the bow and, like the preceding photograph, was taken on 3 October 1938. At the bottom of the ship, with the deck plating yet to be installed, many of the lateral frame members are visible; these are perforated with round openings. (National Archives)

The lateral and longitudinal bulkheads in the aft part of the *North Carolina* take shape on 27 December 1938. The view was taken from around frame 76, in the area where the forward part of the superstructure eventually would take form. (Frames were numbered forward to aft.) The bays between the lateral bulkheads would contain the machinery: boilers, turbines, reduction gears, and so forth. (National Archives)

7

Also taken on 27 December 1938 is this view forward from about frame 84, showing at the bottom the forward bulkheads depicted from the opposite sides in the preceding photograph. The curved fittings at the tops of the vertical frames in the foreground later would provide anchoring points for the horizontal framing of the third deck, which would be constructed of 0.62" armor plate. (National Archives)

On 16 January 1939, the number-four boiler is being lowered into position in the number-two machinery space, facing to starboard. The ship was equipped with eight Babcock & Wilcox double-uptake boilers, rated at 850 degrees Fahrenheit and 575 psi. Two boilers were in each of the four machinery spaces. It was early winter, and the unenclosed hull had a coating of snow. (National Archives)

In a photo taken shortly after the preceding one, the number-four boiler has just landed in place in the number-two machinery space. Another boiler is already in place to the left, and workmen are in the process of setting it up. The Babcock & Wilcox boilers were three-drum, express-type units with twin furnaces. They burned fuel oil, of which about 7,000 tons were carried onboard. (National Archives)

The number-one machinery space was photographed on 16 January 1939 facing to the starboard side, with scaffolding outside of the hull visible to the top. The number-two boiler has been installed. The machinery spaces were numbered from forward to aft. To the right is the number-two machinery space, inside which two faintly visible workmen are standing atop a boiler. (National Archives)

An overhead view of one of the main-battery barbettes of the *North Carolina* documents an experimental hard-surface welding technique used on the upper track of the barbette, upon which the turret would rotate. Readings were taken of distortions on the track; toward this purpose, the man at the center is manipulating a surveyor's transit fastened to a stack of boxes. (National Archives)

As viewed facing from the port side toward the stern from around frame 123 on the third deck in early April 1939, the barbette of turret three is under construction, its large size brought into perspective from the scale of the men working on its side. As work progressed, the sides of the hull would be extended upwards, and construction of the third deck would advance aft. (National Archives)

Moving farther forward on the port side of the hull of the *North Carolina,* a photographer took this view facing the stern on 3 April 1939, with the top of barbette three visible in the distance. Much of the third deck has been completed above the machinery spaces. Cluttering the deck are ladders, compressed air hoses, welding equipment, tools, and other essential gear. (National Archives)

The forward part of the ship is observed on 3 April 1939 from her port side facing toward the bow. The shell of the hull is taking form to the left, with framing for the shell to be constructed from the bottom up. The barbettes of turrets one and two have yet to take shape. The various frame members and bulkhead plates have copious amounts of writing and markings on them. (National Archives)

Another photograph in the series taken from the port side on 3 April 1939 shows the progress of work on the third deck from frame 106 forward to bulkhead 71 in the distance. Toward the lower right is what appears to be a rivet forge. As a safety precaution, temporary guard rails made of 2x4s are positioned around each opening in the deck. (National Archives)

On 5 May 1939, the conical stool of turret two is being lowered into the barbette on the *North Carolina.* The huge assembly had been delivered alongside the *North Carolina* by the floating crane Hercules. The process of lowering an assembly by crane or hoist onto a ship under construction was known in shipbuilding parlance as "landing." (National Archives)

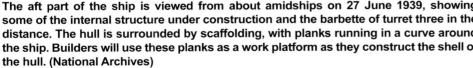

The aft part of the ship is viewed from about amidships on 27 June 1939, showing some of the internal structure under construction and the barbette of turret three in the distance. The hull is surrounded by scaffolding, with planks running in a curve around the ship. Builders will use these planks as a work platform as they construct the shell of the hull. (National Archives)

Also photographed on 27 June 1939 was the forward part of the ship from amidships. Work on the barbettes would proceed, and then the ship's decks would be built around them. Three tiers of wooden scaffolding are arranged around the turret-two barbette, while one tier of scaffolding rings barbette one. Scaffolding also has been erected inside barbette two. (National Archives)

By September 1939, construction of the deck has advanced in the same area depicted in the preceding photograph, showing the barbettes of turrets one and two in the background. To the left of the vertical tube toward the lower right is a solitary workman sweeping the deck; he provides a sense of the vast scale of this shipbuilding endeavor. (National Archives)

Work continues on the aft part of the hull on 27 September 1939. The deck in the foreground, most likely the second deck, is in an advanced state of construction, while the lower decks in the background have yet to be filled in. Stored in circular arrangements at various places on the deck are the oxygen and acetylene bottles used in vast quantities for welding and cutting purposes. (National Archives)

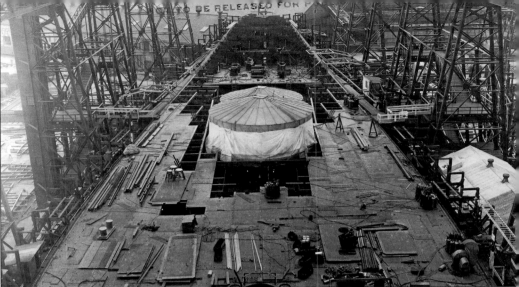

By 28 December 1939, the second deck has been completed past the barbette for turret three, and work has begun on the main deck, with outboard sections being in place. The rings on the sections of main deck represent locations where 5-inch gun mounts will be placed. A temporary, conical cover has been erected over the barbette of turret three to keep the elements out. (National Archives)

The status of work on the forward part of the hull is documented in this photograph dated 1 April 1940. The main deck has advanced to the turret-two barbette. The framing for the main deck has not yet advanced into the forecastle. At the bottom of the photo, small sections of the superstructure deck, or level 01, have been erected where two 5-inch gun mounts will be situated. (National Archives)

A crane casts a long shadow over the main deck of North Carolina in another photograph taken on 1 April 1940, facing aft. Four box-shaped sections, the tops of which will be part of the superstructure deck, have been constructed, and these will form the foundations for 5-inch gun mounts. The circular shapes on the main deck will likewise hold 5-inch gun mounts. (National Archives)

The stern of the North Carolina was photographed on the building ways on 11 June 1940, two days before the ship's launching. Large wooden beams, collectively called shoring, are firmly propped up against the hull to hold it in place. Just before launching, workmen will methodically knock out each of the timbers to ready the ship for sliding down the greased ways. (National Archives)

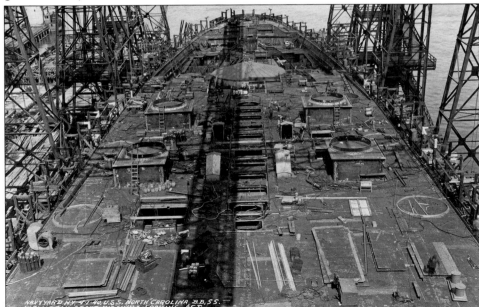

The port side of the stern of *North Carolina* is shown on the day of the ship's launching, 13 June 1940. The white wooden beams and steel I-beams fitted under the contour of the ship are the port after poppet, a temporary structure that supported the weight of the stern. The poppets would remain attached to the ship after launching, to support her during her fitting-out in drydock. (National Archives)

Ballistic Weapons Data

Ammunition type	Mark	Projectile weight	Explosive charge	Muzzle velocity	Range (yards)
16"/45 Armor Piercing	8	2,700 lbs	40.5 lbs	2,300 fps	36,900
16"/45 Armor Piercing	5	2,240 lbs	33.6 lbs	2,525 fps	40,600
16"/45 High Capacity	13	1,900 lbs	153.6 lbs	2,635 fps	40,180
5"/38 High Capacity	35	54 lbs	7.6 lbs	2,600 fps	18,200
5"/38 AAC	35	55 lbs	7.6 lbs	2,600 fps	37,200
40mm Armor Piercing	81	2 lbs		2,890 fps	11,000
40mm AAC	1-2	2 lbs		2,890 fps	22,800
1.1" AAC	1-2	.92 lbs		2,700 fps	19,000
20mm APT	9	.269lbs		2,740 fps	10,000
20mm HE	3	.271lbs		2,740 fps	10,000
20mm HET	7	.271lbs		2,740 fps	10,000

General Data

Length Overall:	728' 8⅝"
Length at waterline:	713' 5¼"
Maximum beam:	108' 3⅞"
Waterline beam:	104' 6"
Mean draft:	31' 7 5/16" @ 42,329 tons
Maximum draft:	35' 6"
Displacement (1942):	36,600 tons Standard
	44,800 tons Full Load

Armor protection:

Main battery turrets: Face plates: 16.0"
Sides: 9.8"
Back: 11.8"
Roof: 7.0"

Barbette Armor: Centerline forward: 14.7"
Sides: 16.0"
Centerline aft: 11.5"

Secondary battery mounts: 1.95"
Magazines: 1.95"

Conning tower armor, Class B: Centerline: 14.7"
Beam: 16.0"
Roof: 7.0"
Communications tube: 14.0"

Belt armor: 12.0" Class A on .75" STS inclined 15°, tapered to 6.6" on .75 Special Treatment Steel (STS)

Deck armor:	Centerline	Outboard
Main:	1.45"	1.45"
Second:	1.4"+3.6"	1.4"+4.1"
Third:	.62"	.75"

Machinery

Boilers: eight Babcock and Wilcox
Geared turbines: four sets General Electric, 121,000 shaft horsepower forward, 32,000 astern

Complement: 2,339 (144 officers, 2,195 enlisted)

Armament – Main Battery: nine 16"/45 caliber Mark 6, model 1937
Secondary Battery: twenty 5"/38 caliber Mark 12, model 1934

Antiaircraft – varies. See table on page 46.

The Launching

The launching of a capital ship is a national event and a cause for national pride, particularly a battleship during the pre-Pearl Harbor era, when a battleship was considered the principal extension of a nation's power overseas. By June 1940, the United States had been without such an event for most of two decades, the result of a moratorium on new battleship construction required by the 1922 Limitation of Naval Armament – commonly called the Washington Naval Treaty. This drought of launchings, and the ebb of national pride due to the Great Depression, made the launch of *North Carolina* especially celebratory.

In addition to the dozens of dignitaries on hand, the launch was watched by the scores of shipyard craftsmen who had formed her hull and complex systems over the previous 32 months. Witness too were throngs New Yorkers who had seen the immense bulk of the ship as it grew in Brooklyn Navy Yard. *North Carolina's* construction was clearly visible from Brooklyn Bridge, and so important was her construction – and the jobs it created – that the Navy repeatedly invited the press to visit the ship during her construction. It was this publicity that would lead the media to dub her "the Showboat," and not, as sometimes reported, frequent trips in and out of the yard to remedy machinery problems – in fact there were no such frequent trips: *North Carolina* only departed New York Harbor four times between late May and late November 1941.

In several days, the *North Carolina* will be launched, and ceremonial platforms to accommodate guests at the launching have been constructed around her hull. The portholes below the main deck would later be covered before the ship was commissioned, to enhance the ship's watertightness. The decoratively painted forward poppets cradle the bow. (National Archives)

This is the *North Carolina's* launching party: the dignitaries that participated in the christening and launching ceremony for the ship. From left to right, they were: Mrs. Padgett, Lt. Sampson, Mrs. Clyde R. Hoey, North Carolina Governor Clyde R. Hoey, Miss Isabel Hoey (the sponsor of the *North Carolina*), Lt. De Metropolis, Mrs. Robinson, and Lt. Myers. (National Archives)

On the afternoon of 13 June 1940, Miss Isabel Hoey, the sponsor of the *North Carolina* and daughter of Governor Clyde R. Hoey of North Carolina, prepares to smash a bottle of champagne on the bow of the ship to christen her. In remarks at the launching, Governor Hoey affirmed that the ship "speaks a language even a dictator can understand," a reference to Axis leaders. (Battleship *North Carolina*)

Just as later in the life of the *North Carolina,* months of training would culminate in a few moments of frantic activity on the battlefront, so too was the launching. Beyond the obvious months of labor to bring the hull of the ship to completion, there was also considerable manpower expended in the act of launching the ship. From 3 a.m. on Tuesday, deliberate steps were taken so that the massive hull would slide gently into the waters on Thursday afternoon. Ashore, 10 officers and 645 shipyard workers labored, while aboard a further five officers, 100 enlisted men and 133 civilians toiled to ensure a smooth and safe launch. Despite – or perhaps because of – such careful planning, the launching of a warship is always a dramatic spectacle.

A view from the port side of *North Carolina* shows how the forward poppets were still secured to the bow to stabilize the forward part of the ship as it moved with increasing momentum down the slippery ways. (National Archives)

Champagne splashes over the bulbous bow of the *North Carolina* as Miss Hoey christens the ship. Mariners have long considered christening with champagne or wine essential to good fortune for the ship. A bulbous bow works to optimize the flow of water around the bow and the ship, reducing drag and improving speed, stability, range, and fuel economy. (National Archives)

The *North Carolina* had been christened, and workers had knocked out the remaining supports to release the ship, when a block on the building ways became wedged, briefly detaining the ship before it was finally sent sliding down the well-greased ways. A band played the U.S. Navy song, *Anchors Aweigh,* as the ship slid into the basin of the Navy Yard, Wallabout Bay. (National Archives)

Accenting the drama of *North Carolina's* launching was the concern that the wars then raging in Europe, and in East Asia, would engulf the United States. Even North Carolina Governor Clyde Hoey, one of the speakers at the event, made a thinly veiled reference to this possibility in his speech.

Once the dignitaries had left the microphone, Governor Hoey's daughter, Isabel, the ship's sponsor, smashed a bottle of champagne on *North Carolina's* bow, christening her. The band struck up "Anchor's Aweigh" and the millions of pounds of steel in the 728-foot long hull rushed down the building ways and into the waters of Wallabout Bay. Soon a bevy of harbor tugs surrounded her hull, itself riding high in the water, and eased her into Drydock Four, to begin her fitting out.

The crowd still looks on as *North Carolina* clears the building ways and, with decreasing momentum, glides out into Wallabout Bay. Framing the scene are the gigantic overhead cranes so essential in constructing the ship. (National Archives)

The *North Carolina* slides stern-first into the water, with the massive cranes of the building ways to the right. On her main deck are the dark forms of the aft fire-control tower and the foundations of the amidships secondary-battery directors. (Battleship *North Carolina*)

When the ship was launched, its engineering system was incomplete: the propellers, for example, would be installed during the fitting-out period. Thus, when the *North Carolina* came to a halt in Wallabout Bay consequent to her launching, an array of tugboats gathered around the ship and towed her to the Drydock No. 4, where she would complete her fitting out. (National Archives)

Powered by a battery of tugboats, the *North Carolina* advances across the basin at the Navy Yard, New York. The forward poppets have been released from under the bow, and the ship is dressed with pennants on overhead lines from stem to stern. Aside from parts of the superstructure deck and two towers for secondary directors amidships, few structures had been built above the main deck. (National Archives)

Tugboats tow the *North Carolina* over the sill of Drydock Four at the Navy Yard, New York, on the day after her launching, to receive her propellers, rudders, and other final touches to the lower hull. Above the red-lead paint on the lower hull is a black band called the boot topping, a plastic-type coating that masked smudges from the oil film that tended to be present in harbors. (National Archives)

The *North Carolina* is secured in Drydock Four, and the water will shortly be pumped out, leaving the ship resting on beams for the next several months. The raised, black area amidships is where the belt armor will be installed during fitting-out. The two "stacks" rising above the main deck amidships are the foundations for the two amidships secondary-battery directors. (National Archives)

At the Navy Yard, New York, on 27 March 1940, several months before the *North Carolina's* launching, the ship's two rudders are upside-down in a furnace following stress-relieving, a process to reduce residual stress in the steel. A feature of these rudders was the angled round opening through the lower part of each one. (National Archives)

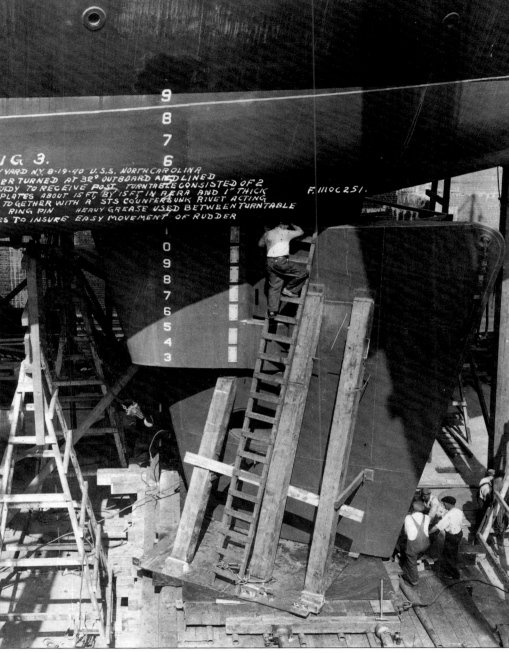

Within the left image:

NY. 8-19-40. U.S.S. NORTH CAROLINA
OLLED INTO PLACE IN RUDDER POST
EEL CABLE ON CORNER OF TURNTABLE
URNING RUDDER AT 32° OUTBOARD ANGLE
DDER STOCK AND CROSS HEAD CAN BE
AS ONE UNIT,
F.1110.G.25.B.

Within the right image:

IG 3.
YARD N.Y. 8-19-40 U.S.S. NORTH CAROLINA
ER TURNED AT 32° OUTBOARD AND LINED
ADY TO RECEIVE POST. TURNTABLE CONSISTED OF 2
PLATES ABOUT 15 FT. BY 15 FT. IN AREA AND 1" THICK
TOGETHER WITH A STS COUNTERSUNK RIVET ACTING
RING PIN HEAVY GREASE USED BETWEEN TURNTABLE
S TO INSURE EASY MOVEMENT OF RUDDER
F.1110 C 251.

Two months after the *North Carolina* was launched, on 19 August 1940, the ship is still in Drydock Four, and the rudders are being installed. A cradle with three braces on each side and situated on a turntable holds the port rudder in position until the connections to the rudder post can be made. The rectangular zinc anodes on the rudder post will help prevent hull corrosion. (Battleship *North Carolina*)

The rudder has been turned 32 degrees to outboard on the turntable in order to seat the rudder on the rudder post. The numbers on the rudder post are draft marks, indicating the distance to the bottom of the keel. Double-digit drafts omitted the first digit. Thus, the 3 on the bottom of the rudder post represents a draft of 13 feet. Draft marks are also on the bow. (Battleship *North Carolina*)

Before the *North Carolina* was launched, full-sized mockups of the interior compartments were constructed at the Navy Yard, New York, in order to test and adjust the layout of components. In this May 1940 view of the mockup of the secondary-battery plot room facing aft, mockups of stable elements are arrayed on the deck to the left; to the right of them are computers. (National Archives)

In this mockup of an interior bulkhead, rough facsimiles of components are fastened to the plywood, each one with an identification label. To the right of the door to the left are several distribution boxes. Even the location of a flashlight has been established to the lower right of the door. Rope is used to show the routing of electrical cables on the bulkhead and overhead frames. (National Archives)

The mockup of the secondary-battery plot is viewed facing forward. Switchboards are to the left, and models of the fire-control computers are placed on the deck. The four computer-stable element units in the secondary-battery plot provided firing solutions for the 5-inch guns against targets on air, surface, or shore. The compartment mockups and contents were largely made of plywood. (National Archives)

Mockups for compartments in the *North Carolina* were also applicable to her sister ship, the *Washington.* This photo is marked as a mockup of both ships' electric deck within a main-battery turret. This deck was located below the gun house in the barbette. Shown is the trainer's station, looking to port. The trainer was tasked with traversing the turret and, thus, the 16-inch guns. (Battleship *North Carolina*)

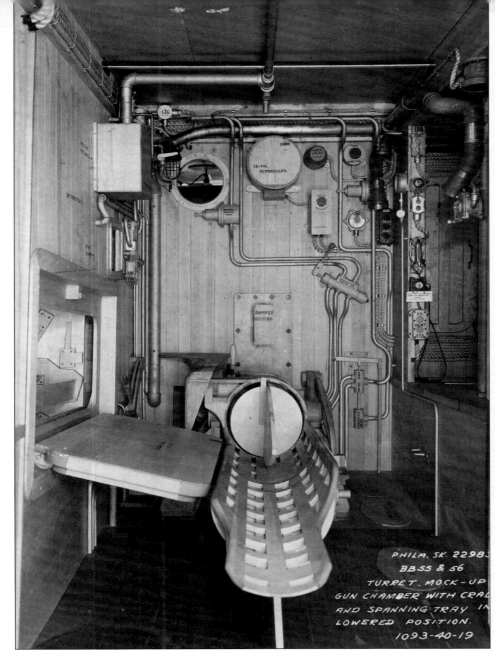

PHILA. SK. 22983
BB 55 & 56
TURRET. MOCK-UP
GUN CHAMBER WITH CRAL
AND SPANNING TRAY IN
LOWERED POSITION.
1093-40-19

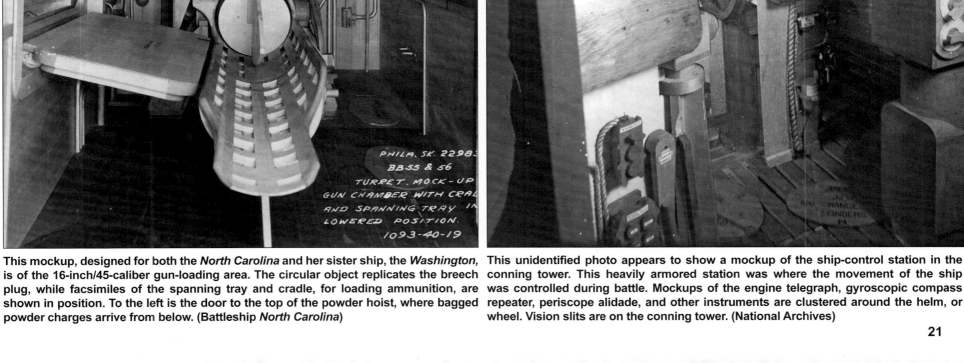

This mockup, designed for both the *North Carolina* and her sister ship, the *Washington,* is of the 16-inch/45-caliber gun-loading area. The circular object replicates the breech plug, while facsimiles of the spanning tray and cradle, for loading ammunition, are shown in position. To the left is the door to the top of the powder hoist, where bagged powder charges arrive from below. (Battleship *North Carolina*)

This unidentified photo appears to show a mockup of the ship-control station in the conning tower. This heavily armored station was where the movement of the ship was controlled during battle. Mockups of the engine telegraph, gyroscopic compass repeater, periscope alidade, and other instruments are clustered around the helm, or wheel. Vision slits are on the conning tower. (National Archives)

Work continues on the fitting-out of the *North Carolina* in Drydock No. 4 at the Navy Yard, New York on 8 August 1940. The view is from the port stern area. Scaffolding has been erected partially alongside the ship, probably for the use of the workers who installed the belt armor along the beams of the ship. Temporary shelters have been installed on the main deck. (National Archives)

The *North Carolina* was photographed from the starboard side on the same day as the preceding photo. Work on the superstructure is advancing; forward of it is the conical cover over the barbette for turret two. Aft of the superstructure are the two foundations for the amidships secondary battery directors. Piled in the foreground are wooden beams and a gangplank. (National Archives)

On 7 September 1940, a 350-ton hammerhead crane lifts turret three of the *North Carolina* preparatory to installing it in its barbette. The forward end of the gun house is open; the faceplate will be installed later, as will be the three 16-inch/45-caliber guns, gun-house roof, after plate, and additional armor. The deck lugs, the cradles that the gun slides' trunnions will rest in, are visible just inside the gun house. The sides of the gun house at this stage comprise thin armor backing plates over which armor plating will be welded once the turret is installed on ship. (National Archives)

Turret three is poised in the air, ready for lowering onto the barbette, around which workmen are standing on the main deck of the *North Carolina*. Details of the underside of the aft overhang of the turret are visible, including two crew-access hatches. The upper cylinder below the gun house was called the gun pit, while the lower, smaller cylinder at the bottom was the electric deck, containing machinery for training (rotating) the turret and elevating the 16-inch/45-caliber guns. The flat surface around the bottom of the gun pit would rest on roller bearings inside the barbette. (National Archives)

At approximately the same moment the preceding photograph was taken, turret three was photographed from a distance off the port stern quarter of the ship, being lowered onto the barbette. The two square openings in the cylindrical bulkhead of the electric deck were where the training pinion would protrude to engage the training rack, encircling the inside of the barbette. Forward of the turret, the aft fire-control tower is taking shape; on top of it are the foundations for the aft fire-control directors. Farther forward, a light-colored funnel is under construction. (National Archives)

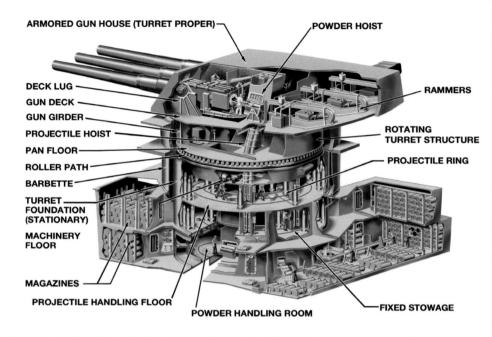

ARMORED GUN HOUSE (TURRET PROPER)

POWDER HOIST

DECK LUG

GUN DECK

GUN GIRDER

PROJECTILE HOIST

PAN FLOOR

ROLLER PATH

BARBETTE

TURRET FOUNDATION (STATIONARY)

MACHINERY FLOOR

MAGAZINES

PROJECTILE HANDLING FLOOR

POWDER HANDLING ROOM

RAMMERS

ROTATING TURRET STRUCTURE

PROJECTILE RING

FIXED STOWAGE

Turret three is slowly being lowered into its barbette; the bottom level of the turret is already inside the barbette. The two crew hatches can be seen on the bottom of the overhang. This plate on the bottom of the gun house is referred to as the shelf plate. (National Archives)

Turret three is now seated and ready for the installation of its equipment, guns, and armor. Visible inside the open aft end of the gun house is the transverse bulkhead. Aft of the bulkhead would be the turret officer's booth. An optical rangefinder would take up much of the space in this compartment. Forward of the transverse bulkhead would be separate compartments for loading each 16-inch gun. Armor was yet to be applied over the gun house: 16" on the face, 9.8" on the sides, 11.8" on the rear, and 7" on the top. (National Archives)

North Carolina's starboard side is seen in this shot of her fitting out in Drydock No. 4 on 30 September 1940. Scaffolding makes the forward fire-control tower resemble a pagoda. The basic structures of the two funnels are in place. A conical cover is over barbette two. In the foreground is the gun house of a 5-inch gun mount. (National Archives)

The forward starboard portion of the *North Carolina* is seen on 30 September 1940. The forward end of the starboard belt armor is clearly visible, with the dark paint or primer it was treated with overlapping the hull color. The belt armor, installed over .75" special treatment steel (STS) and inclined 15°, was 12" thick, tapering to 6.6" at its bottom edge. While normal U.S. practice was for battleship armor to be proof against weapons equal its own, in this case the armor was proof only against 14-inch shells, the size with which the ship was originally to be armed. (National Archives)

The after part of the ship is depicted in a continuation of the preceding photograph. A close examination of these two images and the following one shows that the belt armor has been installed: it is the dark-colored area on the side of the hull. The aft panel of the side armor of turret three has been installed, and an opening has been cut in its upper aft corner to accommodate the optical rangefinder. A small opening also has been cut for a sight-setter's telescope. (National Archives)

A little over two months after the seating of turret three, on 18 November 1940, one of the 16-inch/45-caliber guns destined for that turret is being lifted by two drydock cranes in preparation for installing it in turret three. The gun barrel has yet to receive its breech and be installed in a slide – the cradle with trunnions that supported the gun in the turret and allowed it to recoil. (National Archives)

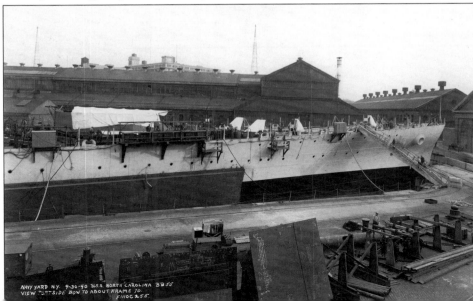

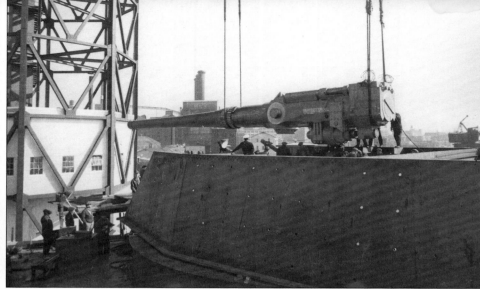

On 9 November 1940, the starboard 16-inch/45-caliber gun in its slide is being lowered onto deck lugs in turret two. The breech is now present on the gun. To the right, work progresses on the forward part of the superstructure and the forward fire-control tower. The part of the superstructure with the semicircular overhang on top is the pilothouse; portholes are yet to be cut. (National Archives)

New York Navy Yard workmen and naval officers are gathered around as the starboard 16-inch gun is almost in place in turret two on 9 November 1940. The trunnion, the cylindrical shape on the side of the gun slide, forms the structural axis around which the gun will elevate. The side of the gun house is still only a backing plate, with the bulk of the side armor yet to be added to it. (Battleship *North Carolina*)

The starboard 16-inch/45-caliber gun was photographed from another angle as it was being lowered into place. On the side of the slide is the port trunnion as well as a stencil identifying it as USS *North Carolina's* right-hand slide for turret two. Secured to the bottom of the slide is the recoil cylinder, the piston of which is fastened to a yoke at the bottom of the breech. (Battleship *North Carolina*)

The gunning of turret three is underway on 18 November 1940. For this turret, a different method of emplacing the gun was used than on turret two, since the gun house of turret three already had its faceplate installed. A 16-inch gun is being lowered onto three cradles on a "runway," temporary tracks on the deck in front of the turret. Then, the gun will be rolled rearward into its slide. (Battleship *North Carolina*)

The center 16-inch gun is being pulled into turret three and is now resting on one cradle, the other two having been removed from the runway as the barrel moved farther into the slide. A system of lines and pulleys was used to pull the gun into the slide. For this method of gun installation, the breech and recoil equipment would be installed once the gun barrel was seated in the slide. (National Archives)

In a view of the starboard side of the *North Carolina* taken on 30 September 1940, a somewhat obstructed view is provided of the bow, with two access ladders set up to accommodate workers. The portholes on the side of the hull, like all others below the main deck, will be covered over by the time the ship is commissioned. Stanchions and guard ropes are installed along the deck. (National Archives)

Seating of the gun in its slide is almost complete, as viewed through the open top of turret three. The next step is to install the yoke, a large unit that acted as a counterbalance and a connection point for the recoil piston and the counter-recoil cylinder yoke rods. The gun fits between longitudinal bulkheads that would protect it from flames and explosions in the other gun compartments. On top of the gun are the two counter-recoil cylinders. A metal bar holds a temporary plug in the breech. The workman at the bottom of the photo provides a sense of the size of the gun's breech. (Battleship *North Carolina*)

The starboard side of the *North Carolina* from the stern to about frame 165 is documented in a photo taken on 30 December 1940. On the fantail are the two turntable-mounted P-6 catapults. The aft fire-control tower is still under construction; atop it are the foundations for the aft main and secondary directors. To the far right is the aft funnel, with scaffolding at the top. (National Archives)

Part of the forward starboard side of the *North Carolina* is depicted on 30 December 1940, from about frame 15 (right) to frame 115 (left). Much scaffolding remains in place on the above-decks structures and the hull. A temporary gable roof has been erected over the gun house of turret two, and aft of that turret, the conning tower is under construction. A single 5-inch gun mount is present. (National Archives)

Virtually the same area of the *North Carolina* as in the preceding photo is shown three months later, on 1 April 1941, eight days before the ship's commissioning ceremony. The ship has received an overall coating of standard U.S. Navy #5 Gray paint. Scaffolding still remains around the aft fire-control tower, and the aft main and secondary directors are yet to be installed. (National Archives)

Three months later, on 1 April 1941, and nine days before the *North Carolina's* commissioning, three more 5-inch gun mounts are present on the starboard side. An interesting detail is the area with scaffolding on the side of the hull where the topcoat of #6 Gray paint has not been applied; permanent covers have been installed over all but a couple of the portholes in that area. (National Archives)

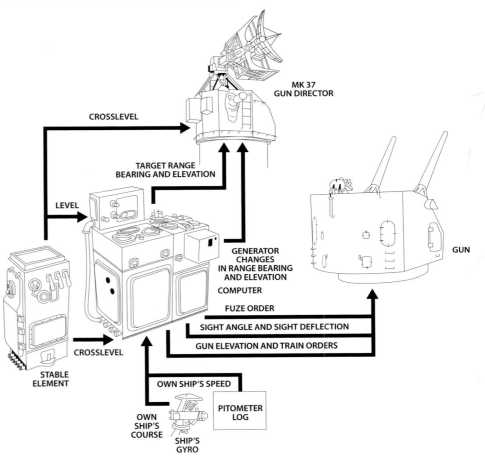

Mk 37 Gun Director

CROSSLEVEL

MK 37
GUN DIRECTOR

TARGET RANGE
BEARING AND ELEVATION

LEVEL

GENERATOR

GUN

CHANGES
IN RANGE BEARING
AND ELEVATION

COMPUTER

FUZE ORDER

SIGHT ANGLE AND SIGHT DEFLECTION

CROSSLEVEL

GUN ELEVATION AND TRAIN ORDERS

STABLE
ELEMENT

OWN SHIP'S SPEED

PITOMETER
LOG

OWN
SHIP'S
COURSE

SHIP'S
GYRO

In a photo taken from the bow of the *North Carolina* on 22 March 1941, the forward Mk. 37 secondary battery director is being lowered toward its mount above the pilot house. The four secondary battery directors on the ship were stations where spotters visually (and later, also with radar) acquired and tracked aerial or surface targets and communicated that information to a plotting room below decks, where that information was processed into firing solutions for the 5-inch guns. The secondary battery directors could also direct the 40mm antiaircraft guns and, in emergencies, the 16-inch main battery. The director comprised a turretlike housing made of 1.5-inch STS (special treated steel). It enclosed a Mk. 42 15-foot optical rangefinder and three Mk. 60 movable prism telescopes. A crew of six, and sometimes seven, manned the Mk. 37 director. In the background are the *North Carolina's* superstructure and fire-control tower, while at the bottom is the temporary roof over turret two.

The Mk. 37 secondary battery director usually was tasked with tracking enemy aircraft and ships, primarily destroyers, and establishing their range, bearing, and, in the case of aircraft, altitude. Those data were transmitted to the plotting room ("Plot"), where analog computers, working with stable elements, which corrected for the pitch and roll of the ship, and the ship's gyro and pitometer, which provided information on the ship's course and speed, calculated within seconds the firing solution for the 5-inch guns. Plot sent that data to the director as well as the 5-inch turret and also controlled the train (traverse) and elevation of both the guns and the director. However, the director also made corrections to the target bearing, range, and angle of attack. Also, although directors normally controlled the aiming and firing of the 5-inch guns, Plot or the gun crews could control the guns when necessary. Plot would control the guns when firing at targets ashore.

This photograph of a nearly complete USS *North Carolina* (BB-55) is dated 17 April 1941, eight days after her commissioning. The ship is resplendent in a fresh coating of standard U.S. Navy #6 Gray paint. On the main deck, partway between the hawse pipe for the port anchor and turret one, is a slight recess in the deck, forming an inclined platform called a billboard for stowing a spare anchor. This feature would later be eliminated during a modernization of the ship. Although the ship had officially entered the service, many details remained to be completed. The portholes were not yet cut in the armor of the pilothouse. Rangefinders were not yet installed in the main-battery gun houses. However, a close examination of the photo shows that the ship's bell had been mounted on the forward face of the fire-control tower. (National Archives)

While the *North Carolina* was built by the New York Navy Yard, and paid for by U.S. taxpayers, she was not truly a U.S. Navy ship until commissioning. Five months ahead of schedule – timing accelerated by fears the nation would soon be involved in the war sweeping Europe – on Wednesday afternoon, 9 April 1941, before 1,000 invited guests, the *North Carolina* was placed in commission, for the first time becoming officially the USS – United States Ship – *North Carolina*.

The relatively modest spectator turnout – crew outnumbered guests – was largely due to concerns about security and sabotage. Most of the guests were Navy officers and their families. Nevertheless, there was considerable enthusiasm among the crew, many of whom had eagerly sought a billet on the Navy's newest battlewagon.

Although now officially a U.S. military asset, much work remained before *North Carolina* would be ready for combat. The ship's fitting out and provisioning required long hours of labor by the crew. Then came sea trials, during which all the ship's systems, from galley to gunnery, were tested.

For many of the original crew – "plank owners" as they proudly call themselves – the most memorable part of the trials occurred on 29 August 1941 when 19 guns – all the 16-inch main battery weapons along with all 10 five-inch guns in her port-side five-inch mounts – were fired simultaneously, hurling 12 tons of steel over the water, in what was up to that time the most powerful broadside ever fired by any navy. Numerous media representatives were aboard for this test, and they, along with the crew, were awed by the immense forces generated.

Secretary of the Navy Frank Knox (left) shakes hands with the ship's first commander, Capt. Olaf M. Hustvedt at the USS *North Carolina's* commissioning at the New York Navy Yard on 9 April 1941. To the right is J. M. Broughton, governor of North Carolina. The commissioning ceremony of a U.S. Navy capital ship was always an important event, marking the Navy's formal acceptance of the vessel into service. This occasion received more than usual attention from the public and the press, since the ship was the first of the Navy's new, fast battleships armed with 16-inch guns, and the first newly designed U.S. battleship to be commissioned in 20 years. Adding an impressive new warship to its inventory, the Navy ended a long moratorium on battleship construction, while the vessel's new crew celebrated their ship's coming-of-age. During the ceremony, the *North Carolina* was entrusted to her commander. (Battleship *North Carolina*)

Another ceremony enacted was stepping the mainmast, in which coins were placed on step, or foundation, of the mainmast for good luck before the mainmast was anchored in place. This practice is thought to have originated with the ancient Romans, either as a sacrificial gesture or to pay the mythological Charon to ferry the ship's crew across the River Styx should they die at sea. (National Archives)

The Stars and Stripes wave from the flag staff of the USS *North Carolina* while the crew and guests witness the commissioning proceedings being conducted on the quarterdeck. Only after a ship is commissioned is she legally the property of the United States government and qualified to bear before her name the designation USS: United States Ship. (Naval History and Heritage Command)

The port P-6 catapult is shown in close detail during the 9 April 1941 commissioning of USS *North Carolina.* Spectators and news cameramen stand on the catapult to get a better view of the ceremony on the quarter deck. The P-6 catapult used a black-powder charge in a special combustion chamber to propel a launch cart to which the plane's center pontoon was attached. (National Archives)

Eight days after her commissioning, USS *North Carolina* was photographed dockside at the Navy Yard, New York, on 17 April 1941. Sky Control, the air-defense officer's battle station, is the platform with splinter shield protruding from near the top of the forward fire-control tower. "Spot 1," the forward Mk. 38 main-battery director, has yet to be installed atop the fire-control tower. (National Archives)

This view from off USS *North Carolina's* starboard stern dated 23 April 1941 shows that all four of the Mk. 37 secondary battery directors had been mounted. However, the Mk. 38 main-battery directors are not mounted yet. The aft Mk. 38 director, called Spot Two, would be located on top of the cylindrical foundation immediately forward of the aft Mk. 37 secondary-battery director. (National Archives)

On the same date as the preceding photograph, USS *North Carolina* was photographed off her port stern at the Navy Yard, New York. Immediately forward of her flag staff is the aircraft-handling crane, which would lift the ship's scout/observation floatplanes off the water after they returned from missions and place them back on the catapults. The port catapult is also in view. (National Archives)

With assistance from tugboats, the *North Carolina* returns to the Navy Yard, New York, after her first builder's trials, from 19 to 21 May 1941. These first at-sea trials conducted after the ship's commissioning were under the command of Capt. O. M. Hustvedt, USN. The purpose of the builder's trials was to assess the seaworthiness of the ship and detect any structural or mechanical problems, so they could be addressed and corrected before the ship entered operational service. The forward Mk. 38 main-battery director is not present; it would not be mounted on top of the forward fire-control tower until 26 May, just before the second builder's trial. (Battleship *North Carolina*)

The *North Carolina* presents her starboard side at the time of the first builder's trials. The ship was then painted overall in standard U.S. Navy #5 Gray paint. A complement of motorized whaleboats and captain's gigs were onboard, stowed adjacent to and aft of the aft funnel. Boat cranes are visible to the sides of the aft funnel. In the background are masts of other vessels. (Battleship *North Carolina*)

Another photograph of the *North Carolina* during her first builder's trials in May 1941 was shot from off her port beam. The foundation of the aft Mk. 38 main-battery director, the taller of the two cylindrical objects aft of the aft funnel, would later be reinforced fore and aft with diagonal structural bracing when it was found that the director suffered from excessive vibration. (Battleship *North Carolina*)

Originally, USS *North Carolina* had two three-bladed propellers in the outboard positions and two four-bladed propellers in the inboard positions, but vibration problems the ship experienced during trials led to studies that resulted in swapping the positions of the three- and four-bladed propellers, to the configuration shown here. The port skeg, on which the inboard propeller was mounted, is shown to good advantage. (Battleship *North Carolina*)

The *North Carolina's* rudders and starboard-side propellers are shown while the ship is in drydock. Although the *North Carolina's* sister ship, the *Washington,* went to war with five-bladed propellers on the inboard positions, the *North Carolina* entered the conflict with the three-bladed inboard propellers, exchanging those for five-bladed propellers during a September 1944 refitting at Puget Sound Navy Yard. (Battleship *North Carolina*)

This original color photo of the USS *North Carolina* shows the battleship conducting military trials during late August 1941. Earlier that month, the original paint scheme of #5 Gray had been overpainted with a Measure 12 camouflage scheme of Sea Blue (5-S) on the hull; Ocean Gray (5-O) on the superstructure; a color that remains controversial, possibly Light Gray (5-L) or Standard Navy Gray, on the top of the forward fire-control tower and the pole masts; and Deck Blue on at least some of the metal parts of the decks. (In photographs of the ship taken in August-September 1941, the top color seems to be too light to have been Haze Gray (5-H), the officially prescribed color.) The teak deck was not painted at this time. The light-colored pattern on the lower part of the bow is not a painted-on false bow wave, but rather the effects of the Sea Blue paint chipping off from the original #5 Gray paint due to hydrodynamic action: the wear and tear that the splashing and churning of water had on paint. (Stan Piet Collection)

The wildcats were chain wheels akin to drive sprockets: they had indentations in the rims matching the contours of the anchor chains, and as the windlasses powered the wildcats, the wildcats gripped the chains, raising or lowering the anchor. From the wildcat, each anchor chain passed down through an opening to the chain lockers. The cover of the opening on the left has been removed. (National Archives)

From the wildcats (upper right), the anchor chains extend forward over steel chafing plates to the hawse pipes; this is the starboard one. When the anchor was raised, its shank was housed in the hawse pipe. A grille covered the upper opening of each hawse pipe; toggle bolts with hex nuts secured the grilles in place. Immediately aft of the hawse pipe is one of the pelican hooks that secure the anchor chain. (National Archives)

NAVY YARD, NEW YORK   AUGUST 1941   U.S.S. NORTH CAROLINA

RADAR ANTENNA NORTH CAROLINA.   F1110-C-483

This photograph dated August 1941 shows technicians working on the CXAM-1 radar antenna on the foremast of USS *North Carolina* at the Navy Yard, New York. Some sources have incorrectly reported that this radar was not installed until toward the end of 1941. Produced by RCA, the CXAM series was the first production type of radars to be installed on U.S. warships. (National Archives)

The forward starboard part of the USS *North Carolina* is detailed in a photo from the summer of 1941. Abrasion of the paint above the waterline at the bow where the Sea Blue paint has peeled off the base coat of #5 Gray paint is apparent. However, the boot topping, the black band along the waterline composed of a durable plastic coating, remains intact and retains its sharply defined, straight top edge. The purpose of the boot topping along the waterline was to hide the film of oil that tended to collect on the hull in virtually any harbor, where oil, leaking from ships and spilled during maintenance operations, usually floated on the surface of the water. (National Archives)

In a companion view to the preceding one, the ship is viewed from amidships to the bow. The chipping of the Sea Blue paint that was so prominent on the bow receded farther aft, but evidence of chipping paint is evident toward the aft end of the hull. (National Archives)

The USS *North Carolina* is viewed from astern in another photograph from the same series of photos. The shape of the aircraft-handling crane on the fantail is silhouetted against the sky, as is the CXAM-1 radar antenna at the top of the foremast. (National Archives)

The light-colored upper part of the forward fire-control tower, possibly painted Light Gray or Standard Navy Gray, contrasts noticeably with the lower part of the tower's Measure 12 scheme of Ocean Gray (5-O). Visible on the roof of turret three is an auxiliary rangefinder, present during the 1941 trials but removed during a subsequent refitting, before the 20mm antiaircraft battery was installed on the rear of the roof of that turret. The ship's Vought OS2U Kingfisher floatplanes were not aboard the ship during this phase of her shakedown cruises. (National Archives)

The aft superstructure, sometimes referred to as the aft fire-control tower, is viewed from the starboard side in a November 1941 photograph. To the upper left is the foundation of the aft Mk. 37 secondary battery director and two 36-inch searchlights. At the upper center is the aft Mk. 38 main-battery director, and adjacent to its foundation is a quad 1.1-inch antiaircraft mount. (Battleship *North Carolina*)

In a view similar to the preceding one, two ladders are installed on the starboard side. Rigged to the aft ladder is a block and tackle extending to the swiveling davit to the far left of the photo, for raising and lowering the ladder. An excellent view is also provided of the belt armor. Hanging over the belt armor forward of the ladder to the left is a hose for discharge water. (National Archives)

An August 1941 view taken at the Navy Yard, New York, shows the starboard forward ladder in place. This ladder would be deployed when boats were embarking or delivering personnel from the ship. The bottom of the ladder is supported by a cable running from a bracket on the side of the hull to the yoke affixed to the ladder. When this photo was taken, between 19 and 21 August 1941, the ship was undergoing a repainting to Measure-12 camouflage. Several sailors are applying Ocean Gray (5-O) to the side of the gun house of turret two; the No. 5 Standard Navy Gray yet to be painted over is to the left of the painters. Below the rangefinder on the side of the gun house and also on the rear of the gun house are ventilation plenums. The hull had been painted Sea Blue (5-S). (National Archives)

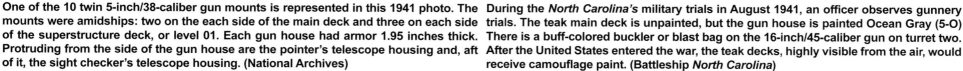

One of the 10 twin 5-inch/38-caliber gun mounts is represented in this 1941 photo. The mounts were amidships: two on the each side of the main deck and three on each side of the superstructure deck, or level 01. Each gun house had armor 1.95 inches thick. Protruding from the side of the gun house are the pointer's telescope housing and, aft of it, the sight checker's telescope housing. (National Archives)

During the *North Carolina's* military trials in August 1941, an officer observes gunnery trials. The teak main deck is unpainted, but the gun house is painted Ocean Gray (5-O) There is a buff-colored buckler or blast bag on the 16-inch/45-caliber gun on turret two. After the United States entered the war, the teak decks, highly visible from the air, would receive camouflage paint. (Battleship *North Carolina*)

Viewed from the forecastle in August 1941, crewmen go about their duties. To the right on a slightly recessed platform, or billboard, is the spare anchor. Partway up the fire-control tower is the demarcation line between the lower color, Ocean Gray (5-O), and the upper color, which, according to the September 1941 "Ships-2" was supposed to be Haze Gray (5-H) but may actually have been a lighter color. (Battleship *North Carolina*)

Turret two has traversed to 90 degrees port as North Carolina undergoes her trials. Interestingly, all three main battery turrets had buff-colored bucklers on the outboard 16-inch guns and black bucklers on the center guns. The brightly holystoned decks visible here are a marked contrast to the subdued camouflage paint that they would wear in only a few months. (Hampton Roads Naval Museum)

The 16-inch/45-caliber guns of turret one are trained to port during firing tests while the USS *North Carolina* is conducting military trials in late August 1941. The "notch" on the port side of the in the foredeck is the recessed platform for stowing a spare Baldt patent anchor. This anchor would first be replaced by an antiaircraft gun, then subsequent refits would see the platform removed altogether. (Hampton Roads Naval Museum)

The face of turret three was photographed from the quarterdeck facing forward during the *North Carolina's* 1941 trials. A military censor has obscured the CXAM 1 radar antenna for security reasons. At the third level above the superstructure deck is a platform for two 36-inch searchlights, above which is the aft, or number-four, Mk. 37 secondary-battery director, turned to port. (Hampton Roads Naval Museum)

The 16-inch/45-caliber guns of turret three have just fired a salvo toward the starboard side during military trials in late August 1941. Firing the main-battery guns was a real test of not only the guns, but also of the structural strength and integrity of the ship. A firing of a salvo by all of the ship's 16-inch guns during a nighttime test in Casco Bay, Maine, proved a success. (Battleship *North Carolina*)

A photographer on another ship caught this impressive view of the USS *North Carolina's* aft main battery firing a salvo during August 1941 military trials. The 16-inch/45-caliber guns were the Mk. 6, a lighter model than the Mk. 1 16-inch guns mounted in the *Colorado*-class battleships, featuring a smaller-diameter breech and a three-hoop barrel, as opposed to the Mk. 1's seven hoops. (Battleship *North Carolina*)

To the right, during *North Carolina's* military trials, is Captain Olaf M. Hustvedt, the ship's first commander (9 April to 23 October 1941). To the left is an unidentified commander. A 1909 graduate of the U.S. Naval Academy, Hustvedt served in both world wars, including as Commander Battleships, Atlantic Fleet, and of Battleship Division 7, achieving the rank of vice admiral. (Battleship *North Carolina*)

The *North Carolina* was equipped with two P-6 powder-propelled, turntable-mounted catapults on the fantail. This is the starboard one. Visible on the forward (left in the photo) end of the catapult are hydraulic bumpers, which cushioned the shock of the launch cart when it reached the end of its travel. Present on deck are various ventilators and hatches. Turret three's guns are to the left. (National Archives)

The destroyer USS *Meredith* (DD-434) crosses astern of the USS *North Carolina* during military trials in the summer of 1941. Two of turret three's 16-inch guns are visible at the bottom of the photograph. To the right of the guns, on the fantail, is the aircraft-handling crane. Two quad-40mm Bofors antiaircraft gun tubs later were mounted on the fantail on each side of the crane. (Stan Piet Collection)

Crewmembers of the *North Carolina* gather on the quarterdeck and atop turret three to observe trials of the ship's Vought OS2U Kingfishers. The plane on the starboard catapult is being prepared for launch, its pilot and radioman/observer in their seats and the catapult aimed into the wind. A crewman dressed in whites is warming the engine of the plane on the port catapult. (Battleship *North Carolina*)

After a Kingfisher has been launched from the starboard catapult and the catapult has been returned to position, the port catapult has been positioned to launch another Kingfisher. On the deck between the center and starboard 16-inch guns of turret three are two floatplane dollies, on which Kingfishers could be stored and moved around on deck, as necessary. (National Archives)

This Vought OS2U-2 assigned to the USS *North Carolina* wears a prewar paint scheme of NS Light Gray. The ship's name is painted in white below the radioman/observer's cockpit. The beaching gear of two main wheels and a tail wheel on the center pontoon allowed for the movement of the plane on land. Vought produced a total of 158 OS2U-2s. (Battleship *North Carolina*)

One of USS *North Carolina's* Vought OS2U-2 Kingfishers is viewed from the front on 12 May 1941. The OS2U was powered by a Pratt & Whitney R-985-48 450-horsepower, nine-cylinder radial engine. It had a top speed of about 170 miles per hour and a range of about 800 miles. Kingfishers would serve on the USS *North Carolina* until the end of World War II. (Battleship *North Carolina*)

The OS2U-2 was outwardly similar to its predecessor, the Vought OS2U-1, but had improvements such as self-sealing fuel tanks, crew armor, and increased fuel capacity, with a carbon dioxide gas-purge system to alleviate the concentration of explosive vapors. (Battleship *North Carolina*)

This Vought OS2U-2 Kingfisher appears in the paint scheme of an aircraft assigned to the USS *North Carolina* during its military trials in the summer of 1941. The first three OS2U-2s assigned to the *North Carolina* at the Navy Yard, New York, reportedly were bureau numbers 2288, 3073, and 3074. Initially, the *North Carolina's* aircraft were not assigned to numbered observation squadrons, but later, Observation Squadron 6 (VO-6) incorporated the Kingfishers of the USS *North Carolina* and USS *Washington*.

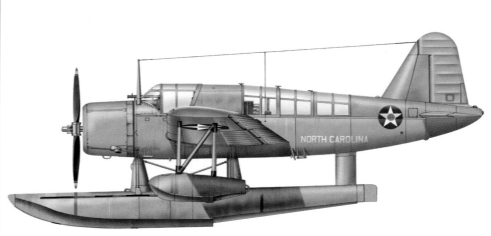

The USS *North Carolina* displays the original Measure 12 paint scheme the ship wore between August and November 1941, when the ship was repainted in a significantly different, modified Measure 12 scheme. The contrast in tones between the Sea Blue on the hull, the Ocean Gray on the superstructure, and the controversial light color on the top of the fire control tower is noticeable. The foundation of the aft Mk. 38 main-battery director still lacks the substantial structural bracing it will receive in its November 1941 refitting. Two captain's gigs and a motorized whaleboat are stored amidships. (National Archives)

Anti-Aircraft Armament

Present as of	Quad Mounts	Oerlikons	Light Machine Guns
April 1941	4 x 1.1" Quad mount		12 x .50 BMG
February 1942	4 x 1.1" Quad mount	40 x 20mm	12 x .50 BMG
June 1942	4 x 1.1" Quad mount	40 x 20mm	26 x .50 BMG
November 1942	10 x 40mm Quad mount	40 x 20mm	
April 1943	14 x 40mm Quad mount	53 x 20mm	
November 1943	15 x 40mm Quad mount	46 x 20mm	
September 1944	15 x 40mm Quad mount	48 x 20mm	
August 1945	15 x 40mm Quad mount	36 x 20mm	

As built, the *North Carolina's* automatic antiaircraft weapons suite included four quadruple 1.1-inch automatic guns and 12 .50-caliber machine guns. Shown here, the quad 1.1-inch mount was designed to combat the aircraft of the 1930s. The guns were water cooled and fired an explosive shell, fed in eight-round clips. Seats, sights, and control hand wheels were provided for the pointer and trainer. Quad 40mm automatic gun mounts later replaced the 1.1-inch gun. (National Archives)

As photographed on the port side of the superstructure deck at the Navy Yard, New York, in August 1941, twelve of these water-cooled Browning M2 .50-caliber machine guns originally were mounted on the USS *North Carolina.* The weapon fired at a rate of up to 700 rounds per minute, firing a mix of ball-type and incendiary ammunition to a maximum range of about 7,400 yards. Fitted over the barrel of the gun is a cooling sleeve through which water circulated, fed by the rubber hoses and the water tank on the deck. The gun was equipped with bicycle-type grips for better maneuverability. This mount is the Mk. 8. (National Archives)

Sky Control was a platform with a splinter guard near the top of the forward fire-control tower. There, the air-defense officer and machine gun officer, working with lookouts, identified and designated enemy aerial targets and communicated that information to the antiaircraft batteries. Lookouts were provided with swiveling, tilting seats with a yoke to hold binoculars steadily. (National Archives)

Several lookout's seats are shown in Sky Control, with the side of the forward fire-control tower to the right. The "perforations" in the sides of the seat backs appear at first glance to be lightening holes in a metal frame, but actually are indentations in the sides of thick foam cushions. Antiaircraft lookouts typically had an assigned sector of the sky to watch. (National Archives)

A Browning M2 .50-caliber water-cooled machine gun is shown on a Mk. 3 mount on the USS *North Carolina* in August 1941. It is fitted with a ring-and-bead sight offset to the right side and an ammunition box on the left side. The .50-caliber machine gun was effective as a close-in defensive weapon against the low-flying, relatively slow aircraft of the 1930s, but by the start of World War II, one dozen of these guns was not an adequate defense for a battleship. Shortly after the United States entered the war, the *North Carolina* would replace its battery of .50-caliber machine guns with 20mm automatic cannons. (National Archives)

Sky Control had four target designators, one of which is shown on the pedestal to the right of center, to provide information on target location and bearing to the antiaircraft batteries. Also in Sky Control were various indicators and communications equipment. In addition to the two aforementioned officers, Sky Control contained a lookout officer, talkers, and lookouts. (Battleship *North Carolina*)

For illuminating aerial and surface targets at night, the USS *North Carolina* carried an array of 24-inch and 36-inch searchlights. This 36-inch searchlight and the one partially visible in the background were among the four located on the searchlight platform amidships, on the same level as the flag bridge. To the left is the foundation of an amidships Mk. 37 secondary battery director. (National Archives)

NAVY YARD, NEW YORK   AUGUST 1941   U.S.S. NORTH CAROL

FROM THE FLAG AND SIGNAL BRIDGE LOOKING AFT SHOWING FROM LEFT TO
FORWARD SMOKEPIPE PORT FORWARD SECONDARY BATTERY DIRECTOR TOWER
RANGE FINDER 36" SEARCHLIGHT PLATFORM AND ITS PORT SEARCHLIGHTS,
PORT FORWARD 5" TURRET ONE GUN SHOWING, THE FLAG BOARD (CANVAS CO
WITH PIN RAIL AND HALYARDS, CORNER OF WINDSHIELD.   F1110-C-489

The two searchlights on the port side of the amidships searchlight platform are viewed from the signal bridge facing aft. A good view is provided of the port amidships Mk. 37 director and its foundation. Protruding from the sides of the director is the 15-foot rangefinder. On the face of the director are three protective flaps for the pointer's, trainer's, and control officer's telescopes. Above each of those hatches was a spotting hatch. Grab rails and foot rails were also provided on the exterior of the director. To the left is the forward funnel. (National Archives)

The aft port side of the *North Carolina's* signal bridge is seen on August 1945, with the forward funnel (left) and foundation of the port amidships Mk. 37 director in the background. The signal bridge is where the signal flags, stored in the "flag bag" (also occasionally called the "signal flag board") seen in the foreground, were run up halyards, which are also visible here. There was a similar flag bag on the starboard side of the signal bridge. (National Archives)

Jutting out from each side of the searchlight platform, between the forward and aft 36-inch searchlights, was a small platform for a 12-inch signaling searchlight on a yoke-type pivoting mount. On the side of the light housing is a blinker handle. To the bottom right is the top of 5-inch turret, while the curved rear of the gun house of another 5-inch turret is in the background. (Battleship *North Carolina*)

USS *North Carolina* was armed with 10 Mk. 28 dual 5-inch/38-caliber gun mounts. This mount is under construction at the Naval Gun Factory, Washington Navy Yard, in March 1943, with another 5-inch/38-caliber mount visible in the background. An elevating arc, actuated by elevating pinions to elevate or depress the guns, is visible on the inboard side of each gun. The enclosure for the mount, called the shield, will be installed later. The part of the turret enclosed by and inclusive of the shield was called the gun house. (Naval History and Heritage Command)

The starboard navigation bridge was photographed facing forward in August 1941. In the distance is the door to the pilothouse. To the right of it is an alidade, an instrument for taking bearings to objects. Toward the lower right is a stand for the captain's target designator, which is yet to be installed. At the lower left is a pump for a quad 1.1-inch gun cooling water tank. (National Archives)

This August 1941 view from the port side of the signal bridge shows, left to right, a stand for a 1-meter rangefinder (not yet installed); an alidade (partially hidden behind the post); 12-inch signal light; and the port side of the flag bridge in the distance, with round portholes. To the right is the armored signal shelter with a vision slot, over which is a hinged cover for the slot. (National Archives)

In an August 1941 view of the forward and starboard sides of the pilothouse, mounted on the floor in the foreground are, left to right, the truck and speed light controller, double-ended engine-order telegraph, indicator, binnacle, two gyro repeaters, and the steering wheel. On the starboard bulkhead in the background is a folding chart table, shown in the raised position. (National Archives)

The pilothouse is viewed facing the port forward corner in a November 1941 photo. A captain's chair is mounted to the deck on each side of the compartment. Mounted below the porthole to the far right and the one to the far left are compass repeaters. Other indicators and instruments are above the forward portholes. Removable floor panels have recessed handles. (National Archives)

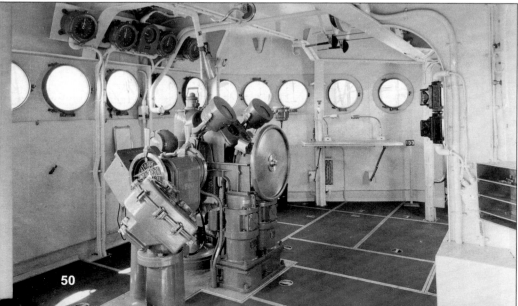

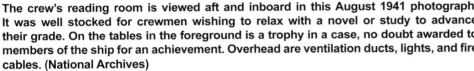

The crew's reading room is viewed aft and inboard in this August 1941 photograph. It was well stocked for crewmen wishing to relax with a novel or study to advance their grade. On the tables in the foreground is a trophy in a case, no doubt awarded to members of the ship for an achievement. Overhead are ventilation ducts, lights, and fire cables. (National Archives)

In another August 1941 interior view of the *North Carolina,* a mess compartment is fitted out with chaplain's effects, complete with a small organ. Typically, religious services were conducted in the mess compartment aft on the starboard side. Attendance at religious services was noticeably higher when the crew was aware that the ship was soon to go into combat. (Battleship *North Carolina*)

Feeding the crew of the *North Carolina* was a critical task, and the ship's galley crews did it well. This view of the crew's galley, facing starboard and aft, shows the bank of three-deck roasting ovens (left), a steam table (center), a fry kettle, a sink and drainboard, and, in the right foreground, five griddles with a storage shelf below it and a pot rack above it. (National Archives)

A mess compartment is shown. Movable, folding, picnic-style tables and seats are arrayed on the floor. The tables have raised rims to keep dishware and other items from sliding off if the ship began to roll or pitch. Along the sides of the compartment are fixed tables with pivoting single seats below them. To the upper right are racks for storing the movable tables when not in use. (Battleship *North Carolina*)

An August 1941 photo shows the secondary-battery plotting room, facing aft. This is where information from the secondary-battery directors was processed into firing solutions for the guns. In the row to the left are four stable elements, while to the right are four fire-control computers. To the right is the fire-control switchboard. The floor panels were removable. (National Archives)

The North Carolina was staffed with expert medical personnel, capable of performing ordinary and emergency surgical procedures. This is the operating room facing aft in August 1941. In the foreground is an operating table, with spotlights overhead. In the background are an instrument cabinet, an instrument and dressing stand, medicine cabinets, lockers, and a fan by the door. (National Archives)

Interior communications central, viewed to port, was manned by electrician's mates of E Division who monitored and repaired the ship's internal communications system. They also maintained the master gyrocompass, partially visible behind the white fixture to the right. To the left is the gyrocompass switchboard. There were also subsidiary interior communications stations throughout the ship. (National Archives)

The front of the lower level of boiler number seven is shown in this November 1941 photograph taken at the Navy Yard, New York. Contrast this view with earlier photos of the number-four boiler being lowered into place almost two years earlier. Once the boilers had been installed, a complicated maze of controls and lines had to be installed to make the boilers operational. (National Archives)

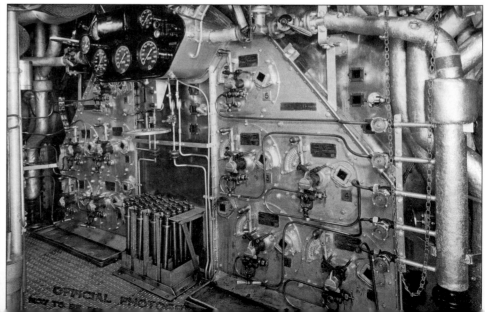

A 16-inch projectile hoist is at the center of this October 1941 photo of one of the *North Carolina's* projectile flats, a compartment deep down in the turret where projectiles are stored and prepared for hoisting up to the gun house. The projectiles were stored on their bases on ring-shaped platforms on the outside and inside of the projectile flat. Three hoists, one for each gun, were on a ring-shaped platform between the outer and inner rings, arranged so that even as the turret moved in train, the hoists remained fixed with respect to the orientation of the gun house. Capstans and lines were used to move projectiles from their storage places to the hoist in a process called parbuckling. (National Archives)

Two levels below the projectile flat in each 16-inch turret was a powder handling room, where bags of ammunition propellant were brought in from magazines, placed on their sides in the hoist shown in this October 1941 photograph, and then sent up to the gun house. There were three powder hoists per turret: one for each gun. Once the powder bags arrived at the top of the hoist, crewmen in a gun-loading compartment opened the door of the hoist and rolled the bags into a tray, where they were rammed into the breech of the gun behind the already loaded projectile. To the left is the central column of the turret, which continued upward to the bottom of the machinery deck. (National Archives)

This is the lower ammunition hoist compartment in USS *North Carolina's* 5-inch/38-caliber mount number nine, looking forward, in October 1941. Here, below the gun house, ready projectiles (left) for the two 5-inch guns were stored before being sent up the hoists to the guns. At the center is the port hoist, and the starboard hoist is to the right. (National Archives)

A crew's mess, compartment C-205-IL, on the second deck between frames 157 and 164, is portrayed in April 1942. Fixed tables with individual stools are attached to the bulkheads, and extra berthing in the form of folding cots is above the tables. Sleeping conditions in the ship were hot, and bedding was aired on deck whenever possible. (National Archives)

This view facing forward inside the gun house of a Mk. 28 5-inch mount taken in October 1941 at the Navy Yard, New York, shows the space between the two guns. Toward the outer sides of the photo are the gun slides, inboard of which are the inboard sides of the gun carriages and trunnions. The two vertical structures toward the center are powder hoists; projectile hoists were directly forward of them. Powder cartridges and projectiles were hoisted up to the gun house, where loaders inserted them into the breeches of the two guns preparatory to firing. (National Archives)

In November 1941, the USS *North Carolina* underwent modifications at the Navy Yard, New York. A repainting in a modified Measure 12 camouflage scheme was part of this work. This scheme called for a mix of areas of Ocean Gray (5-O), Haze Gray (5-H), and Navy Blue (5-N) on vertical surfaces, and Deck Blue (20-B) on all decks and horizontal surfaces. Other modifications implemented on the ship during her November 1941 stay at the Navy Yard, New York, included the installation of radar antennas on the main-battery and secondary-battery directors, and the construction of heavy braces to the fore and aft of the foundation of the aft Mk. 38 main-battery director. (Battleship *North Carolina*)

The port side of the above-decks portion of the citadel, the armored forward superstructure, is displayed in this photo taken during USS *North Carolina's* November 1941 refitting. The contours of the modified Measure 12 scheme are visible. To the far left is the conning tower, aft of which are, from the main deck upward, the officers' mess, captain's quarters, admiral's quarters, flag plot, pilothouse, and forward Mk. 37 secondary battery director, called Spot One. The frame for a Mk. 4 radar antenna has been fitted on top of that director. Aft of that director is the forward fire-control tower, topped with the Mk. 38 main battery director, which has just been fitted with a Mod. 1 Mk. 3 main battery fire-control radar antenna. Jutting from the tower below the Mk. 38 director is Sky Control, the air-defense battle station. Atop the mainmast is the CXAM 1 radar antenna. (Battleship *North Carolina*)

The port amidships area of the *North Carolina* is shown in November 1941 during the ship's refitting at the Navy Yard, New York. Flanking the forward funnel are the two amidships Mk. 37 secondary battery directors, each of which has a frame on top for a soon-to-be-installed Mk. 4 radar antenna. A platform for 36-inch searchlights is around the lower part of the funnel and the foundations of the Mk. 37 director foundations. Motorized whaleboats are stacked one on top of the other between the funnels. Details of three of the 5-inch gun mounts are visible. To the far right is the port boat crane. Behind the rear arm of the crane is the aft Mk. 38 main battery director, called Spot Two. The slanted braces that had just been added to the front and rear of this director's foundation are visible. Atop Spot Two, a Mod. 1 Mk. 3 fire-control radar antenna has been installed. (Battleship *North Carolina*)

As can be seen in this photo of the *North Carolina* from amidships facing aft in November 1941, the newly installed forward bracing on the foundation of the aft main battery director consisted of two triangular bulkheads spaced apart, with a single X-brace between them. The captain's gig is resting in metal cradles fitted to the gunwales of the motor whaleboat beneath it. A fire-control radar antenna has not yet been installed on top of the aft Mk. 37 secondary battery director. A 36-inch searchlight is on the platform next to the foundation of the Mk. 37 director. A mix of naval personnel and civilian shipyard workers are present on the deck. (Battleship *North Carolina*)

In this view of the aft part of the *North Carolina* taken from a platform below the aft searchlight platform, turret three displays an auxiliary rangefinder at the rear of the roof. That rangefinder was temporarily mounted during the shakedown period. Life rafts are stored on top of the gun house and on the side of the superstructure to the lower left. (Battleship *North Carolina*)

The forward port side of the *North Carolina* is displayed in a photo documenting work done on the ship at the Navy Yard, New York, in late 1941. To the far right, on top of the conning tower, is a Mk. 40 standby rangefinder that had not been present during the ship's August 1941 military trials. The curved objects on the side of the first level of the superstructure are ammunition davits. (Battleship *North Carolina*)

This stunning downward view of the forward part of USS *North Carolina* was taken at the Navy Yard, New York, in November 1941. At the bottom center is the top of the forward Mk. 37 director, with a frame for a radar antenna. Aft of turret two is the top of the conning tower and the Mk. 40 rangefinder. Teak planking is present on the superstructure deck as well as the main deck beyond. (Battleship *North Carolina*)

The USS *North Carolina* rides at anchor off the Navy Yard, New York, on 11 December 1941. Several temporary booms are set up on the foredeck, and turret one is traversed to the starboard side. Frames for radar antennas are installed on top of the forward and two amidships Mk. 37 secondary battery directors, but not on the aft Mk. 37 director; initially, a radar was not mounted on the aft director because it was thought that it would interfere with the radar on the aft main-battery director. The port boat crane is in the process of either lowering or taking on board a motor whaleboat. (Battleship *North Carolina*)

In this second of two rare views of the *North Carolina* taken off the Navy Yard, New York, on 11 December 1941, it is evident that the contours of the darker color on the hull, Navy Blue, were continued on the lower sides of the two 5-inch gun mounts on the main deck. There is a new triangular bracing on the foundation of the aft main-battery director. The United States had entered World War II only a few days earlier, and soon the new battleship would be sent into harm's way to prove her merits and those of her crew. (Battleship *North Carolina*)

The USS *North Carolina* is seen from above as she undergoes a refitting at the Navy Yard, New York, on 19 February 1942. The view incorporates much of the ship from turret one to the stern, and documents the installation of 20mm automatic gun mounts with shields and deck-mounted splinter shields at various places on the ship. For example, three mounts are on each side of turret two, with two mounts lacking splinter shields just aft on each side of the main deck. Two 20mm mounts are behind splinter shields toward the forward end of the superstructure deck. Also, the Mk. 4 antennas now have been mounted on the forward and amidships Mk. 37 directors.

The bow of the *North Carolina* is seen at the Navy Yard, New York, on 19 February 1942. A 20mm automatic gun mount within a C-shaped splinter shield is on each side of the forecastle. Four more 20mm guns are farther aft on the foredeck, with only the aft port gun having a splinter shield; this gun and shield were located in the recessed platform that formerly served as the spare-anchor storage site. Between that mount and the wildcats were six new .50-caliber machine gun mounts, three per side. The decks, including the teak planking, had finally been painted Deck Blue. (National Archives)

The port forecastle 20mm gun mount and splinter shield were photographed on 19 February 1942. Hanging below the receiver of the gun is a spent-brass collector bag. To the left of center is a ready-ammunition box for the 20mm mount. To the far left is a 20mm gun mount lacking a deck-mounted splinter shield. Two hatches are in the center and left foreground. (National Archives)

Continuing the series of photos taken of the USS *North Carolina* at the Navy Yard, New York, on 19 February 1942, in the foreground are the two starboard 20mm gun mounts on the foredeck that lacked deck-mounted splinter shields. Between the two 20mm gun mounts are two 20mm ready-ammunition boxes. To the right is the row of starboard .50-caliber machine gun mounts. (National Archives)

The farthest aft of the three 20mm gun mounts on the forecastle and foredeck was this one, slightly recessed on the platform where the spare anchor formerly was stowed. The view is from the center of the foredeck facing outboard. The mount was partially enclosed by a splinter shield, and two 20mm ready-ammunition boxes were also inside the splinter shield. The 20mm gun is resting at full elevation. The hand wheel on the pedestal of the mount was used to raise or lower the carriage of the gun; raising the carriage and the gun gave the gunner a better means of aiming the gun at higher angles of elevation. (National Archives)

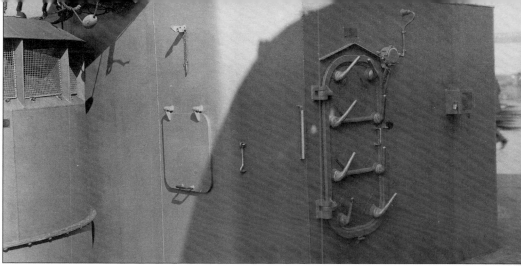

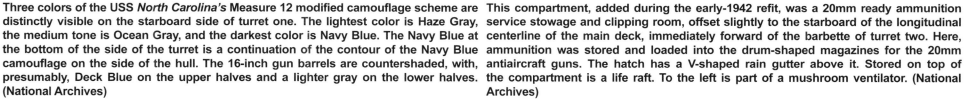

Three colors of the USS *North Carolina's* Measure 12 modified camouflage scheme are distinctly visible on the starboard side of turret one. The lightest color is Haze Gray, the medium tone is Ocean Gray, and the darkest color is Navy Blue. The Navy Blue at the bottom of the side of the turret is a continuation of the contour of the Navy Blue camouflage on the side of the hull. The 16-inch gun barrels are countershaded, with, presumably, Deck Blue on the upper halves and a lighter gray on the lower halves. (National Archives)

This compartment, added during the early-1942 refit, was a 20mm ready ammunition service stowage and clipping room, offset slightly to the starboard of the longitudinal centerline of the main deck, immediately forward of the barbette of turret two. Here, ammunition was stored and loaded into the drum-shaped magazines for the 20mm antiaircraft guns. The hatch has a V-shaped rain gutter above it. Stored on top of the compartment is a life raft. To the left is part of a mushroom ventilator. (National Archives)

The interior of the 20mm ammunition ready ammunition service stowage and clipping room is viewed facing the aft port corner in a 19 February 1942 photograph. The clipping table is in the foreground, with a 20mm ammunition magazine on its far corner. The bulkhead in the left half of the photo is actually the front of the barbette of turret two. (National Archives)

Three 20mm antiaircraft guns and deck-mounted splinter shields were installed on the main deck on each side of turret two during the early-1942 refit. This trio of guns was on the port side. The outboard side of the splinter shield was reinforced with triangular braces. Also behind the splinter shield were ready-service boxes for 20mm ammunition. (National Archives)

As seen in a 19 February 1942 photo, on each side of the superstructure deck between frames 75 and 81, two 20mm antiaircraft guns were installed behind a deck-mounted splinter shield during the early-1942 refit. Two ready-service 20mm ammunition boxes are placed against the superstructure. In the background is 5-inch gun mount number two. (National Archives)

Atop the front of the pilot house of the *North Carolina*, this 20mm gun was installed inside a splinter shield made of 15# special treated steel (STS) in early 1942. Previously, an auxiliary rangefinder had occupied this space. Also in view are a 20mm ready-service ammunition box and, to the right, a pedestal and cradle for a .50-caliber antiaircraft machine gun mount. (National Archives)

These two 20mm antiaircraft gun mounts were added in early 1942 to the main deck, port side, between frames 73 and 86. A similar arrangement of 20mm guns was on the opposite side of the ship. At this time, these guns did not have a deck-mounted splinter shield. In a later refit, one more 20mm gun would be installed in this area, as well as a splinter shield. In the far left background are two pedestal mounts for .50-caliber antiaircraft machine guns, and farther aft is the rear of the shield of 5-inch gun mount number four, the forwardmost 5-inch gun mount on the main deck. (National Archives)

64

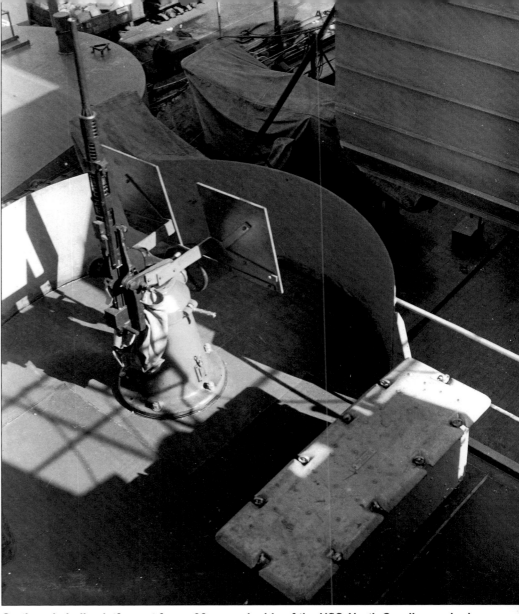

The aft half of the *North Carolina* appears in an overhead photo taken at the Navy Yard, New York, probably in February 1942. A close-up view is offered of the CXAM-1 air-search radar on the foremast and the Mk. 3 Mod. 1 fire-control radar antenna on top of the forward Mk. 38 main-battery director at the lower left. A glimpse is also provided into Sky Control, the platform with a splinter shield below the forward Mk. 38 director. On top of the two amidships Mk. 37 secondary-battery directors are Mk. 4 fire-control radar antennas. The contours of the Measure 12 modified camouflage on the two funnels are apparent. (Battleship *North Carolina*)

On the admiral's platform at frame 96 on each side of the USS *North Carolina,* a single 20mm gun mount was added inside a splinter shield in early 1942. This mount was on the port side, facing forward. The splinter shield was fabricated from 15# STS. To the side is a 20mm ready-service ammunition box, the lid of which was secured in place with 10 latches: one on each end and four on each of the long sides. On the main deck below, the two objects under canvas covers are twin 5-inch loading machines, which generally replicated the structures of the real 5-inch guns and allowed the gun crews to practice loading. (National Archives)

On the level above the chart house and pilot house, as seen in this 19 February 1942 photo facing aft, a 20mm ready-service ammunition stowage and clipping room was installed, abutting the front of the forward fire control tower. The small placard above the rain gutter over the entry hatch identifies the location of the compartment by the level above the main deck, 05, and the frame number, 82. To the side is a locker; there was a similar one on the opposite side of the level. (National Archives)

As built, the *North Carolina* had a Mk. 35 rangefinder on a small platform projecting above the front of the pilothouse. The rangefinder is viewed from aft in an August 1941 photo, showing the two doors on the enclosure's rear, each with two latches. (National Archives)

On the flag and signal bridge, between the two funnels, this house was built to support the number-one radio direction finder. The view is facing aft and was taken on 19 February 1942. A porthole is in the front of the house and an entry hatch is on the side. In the foreground is a walkway between the signal flag bags, the port one being visible to the lower right. In the right background is the foundation of the starboard amidships Mk. 37 director. The forward funnel is to the right. (National Archives)

During the *North Carolina's* early-1942 refit at the Navy Yard, New York, the two aft 36-inch searchlights were removed from the searchlight platform abeam the forward funnel, and a 20mm gun with a splinter shield was installed in each position. In the background of this 19 February 1942 view are stacked life rafts, the aft Mk. 38 main-battery director, and the starboard boat crane. (National Archives)

This splinter shield and the three 20mm guns it protects are emplaced toward the starboard side of the main deck, from abeam the rear of turret three's barbette to just forward of the starboard catapult. A similar 20mm gun emplacement was on the opposite side of the deck. Also visible within the confines of the splinter shield are 20mm ready-service ammunition boxes. (National Archives)

This 20mm ready-service and clipping room is between frames 119 and 121 on the main deck along the centerline of the ship. The clipping table, where the magazines were loaded, is in the foreground. On the bulkhead to the right are stored 20mm ammunition magazines. The fronts of the magazines are facing the camera, and toward the bottoms of them are grab handles. (National Archives)

The aft superstructure is viewed from atop turret three, facing forward, on 19 February 1942. The auxiliary rangefinder on the turret roof had been removed, and three 20mm guns protected by a splinter shield were installed toward the rear of the roof. In the background on each side of the superstructure are quad 1.1-inch gun mounts with splinter shields. (National Archives)

Three .50-caliber machine guns, on what appear to be Mk. 8 mounts, are arrayed on the main deck, facing aft, with the forward gun being abeam of the rear of the aft superstructure. A .50-caliber gun is lying on the deck next to the cooling water reservoir at the center foreground. The spotlight on the stanchion to the left was likely for illuminating the area for workmen at night. (National Archives)

This Mk. 3 gun mount is emplaced on the third level above the superstructure deck adjacent to the foundation of the aft Mk. 38 main-battery director. A similar mount was also placed on the opposite side of that level. Although the original caption states that this was for a .30-caliber machine gun, the intention may have been to mount an M2 .50-caliber machine gun. Toward the top of the mount is the cradle upon which the machine gun will fit. The foundation of the aft Mk. 38 director's foundation is in the background, with the ladder rungs. The aft brace of the director foundation, with a lateral brace on each of its sides, is just beyond the machine gun mount. (National Archives)

Three 20mm guns installed on the fantail during the early-1942 refit are showcased in this 19 February 1942 view. An aft-facing splinter shield has been fitted for each pair of 20mm guns. A close examination of the photo reveals five 20mm ready ammunition lockers. The lower part of the aircraft-handling crane is also in view, as is the flag staff, with its A-shaped split lower legs. To the right are several mushroom ventilators. (National Archives)

This small-arms magazine compartment below decks in the aft part of the ship between frames 138 and 144 is stocked with wooden boxes containing 20mm ammunition. The view is facing forward. Locating the ammunition magazines deep in the hull protected the ship's huge stores of highly explosive ammunition from detonating except by a direct hit. (National Archives)

This 20mm gun mount, the shield of which is visible in the background of the preceding photo, was installed on the starboard side of the main deck at frame 149. The photo was taken at the Navy Yard, New York, on 19 February 1942. In the center background are two 20mm ready-service ammunition boxes, aft of which, next to the aircraft crane, is another 20mm gun mount, the gun pointing straight upward. To the left is the starboard catapult, showing details of its front end and the two hydraulic bumpers. (National Archives)

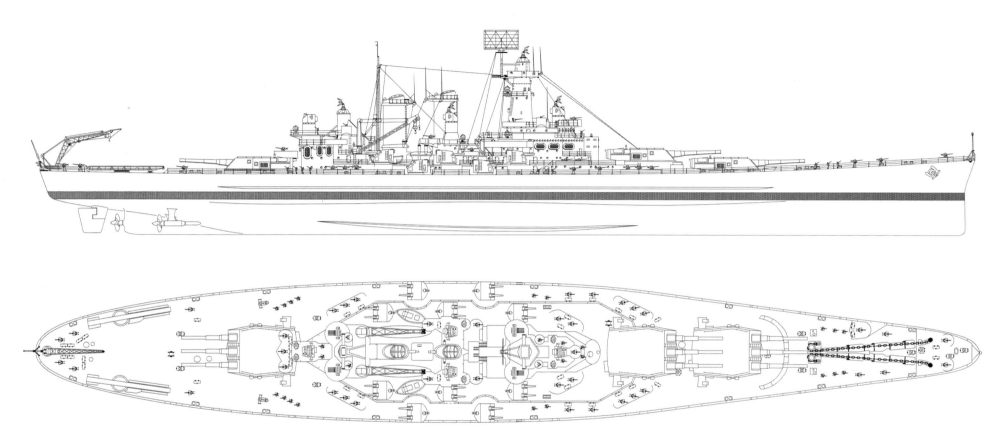

Antiaircraft Armament:	Heavy Machine Gun Battery:	sixteen 1.10"/75 caliber Mark 2, arranged in four quadruple mounts - installed at New York Navy Yard in February 1942.
	Light Machine Gun Battery:	twelve .50 Browning Machine Guns, single mount.
	Medium Machine Gun Battery:	forty 20mm Mount, Mark 2, single - installed at New York Navy Yard in February 1942.

Gun Directors:	Main Battery:	two Mark 38
	Secondary Battery:	four Mark 37
	1.1 Battery:	two Mark 51

Radar:	Search Radar:	CXAM-1
	Main Battery Fire Control Radar:	two Mk 3
	Secondary Battery Fire Control Radar:	three Mk 4 - not installed on aft M37 battery director.

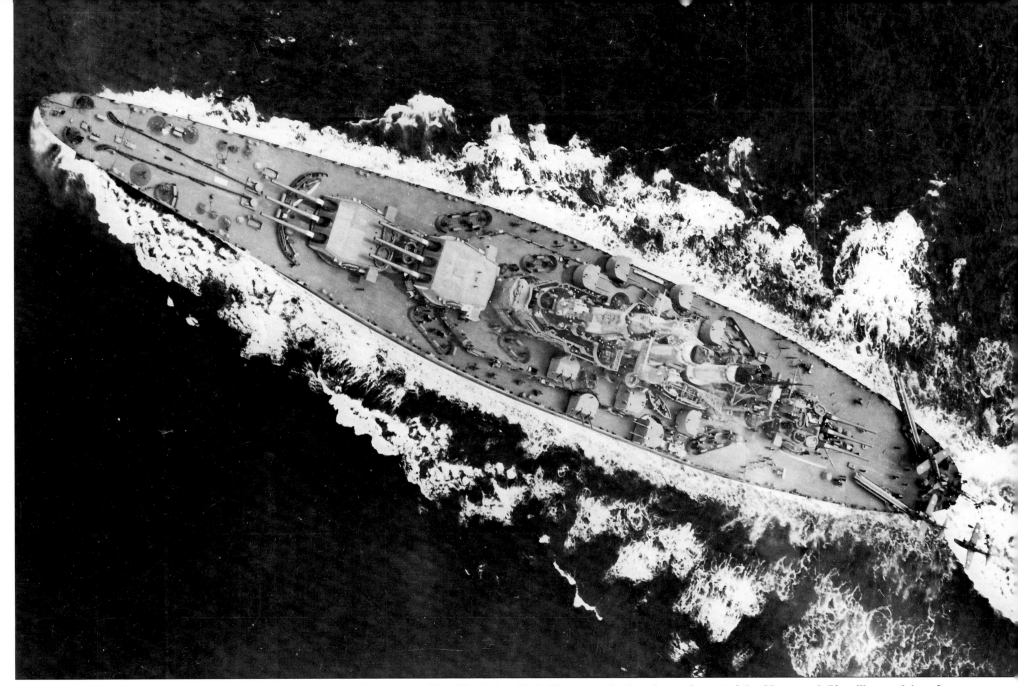

An aerial view of the USS *North Carolina* after its early-1942 refitting at the Navy Yard, New York, illustrates the locations of most of the 20mm and .50-caliber antiaircraft guns and related splinter shields recently installed on the ship. An OS2U Kingfisher is about to be launched from the starboard catapult, while the aircraft-handling crane is bringing aboard another OS2U. (National Archives)

North Carolina's three OS2U Kingfishers are visible on the fantail in this view, with one stowed between the catapults on a dolly. Just visible are the 20mm and .50 caliber machine guns that dot the afterdeck, as well as the trio of 20mm guns and their ammunition lockers atop turret three. Numerous life rafts of various sizes are stowed on the superstructure and 16-inch turrets.

The *North Carolina* visits the Norfolk Navy Yard, Virginia, on 3 June 1942 during its transit from New York to the Pacific. The ship's number, 55, is painted aft of the port hawse pipe. Amidships, crewmen on scaffold planks perform work on the hull, perhaps paint touchups. The ship has its full complement of three OS2U floatplanes, one of them being stored sideways aft of turret three. (National Archives)

The *North Carolina* is viewed from off its starboard stern while at the Norfolk Navy Yard on 3 June 1942. Crewmen dressed in whites are lined up on the main deck, ready to descend the aft ladder into the awaiting boat to take them ashore on liberty. The OS2U on the starboard catapult wears the side number 6-O-6, standing for the sixth aircraft of Observation Squadron 6 (VO-6). (National Archives)

As seen from astern at Norfolk on 2 June 1942, boat booms are deployed, each of which is braced by a stay running from the top of a kingpost on the hull and is equipped with sea ladders by which personnel would climb up to or down from the boom. A catwalk atop the boom provided access to the main deck. An OS2U stored on deck between the catapults has the side number 6-O-4. (National Archives)

A close examination of this photo of the *North Carolina* reveals the various new 20mm gun emplacements and splinter guards. These weapons would soon give the ship a much greater advantage over her original configuration of weapons, but only when the 40mm guns were installed later would the ship attain her full antiaircraft defensive potential. (National Archives)

North Carolina was painted in camouflage Measure 12, modified from November 1941 through November 1942. This scheme featured 5-H Haze Gray as the lightest color, 5-N Navy Blue as the darkest color, and 5-O Ocean Gray as the intermediate color. The decks were finished in 20-B Deck Blue.

The *North Carolina* is in an unidentified port, with a good portion of her crew on deck dressed in whites. The ship's Measure 12 Modified camouflage scheme is apparent, dating the view sometime between November 1941 and November 1942. Two Vought OS2U Kingfishers are resting on the catapults, and the ship's third OS2U is faintly visible sitting on the quarterdeck. (Battleship *North Carolina*)

One of the USS *North Carolina's* Vought OS2U Kingfishers, number 8, is seen in flight. The pilot wears a flight helmet, while the radioman/observer is wearing a cap with headphones over it. The *North Carolina's* Kingfishers and their crews tirelessly flew spotting, scouting, observation, and rescue missions, even losing one aircraft during a rescue attempt. (Battleship *North Carolina*)

Vought OS2U Kingfisher number 8 of the *North Carolina* taxis on a relatively calm stretch of water off a beach while the radioman/observer stands next to the pilot's cockpit. At certain times when the ship was in port or in a harbor, the Kingfishers would fly off and leave the ship for a base on land, where they would undergo repairs, modifications, and maintenance, and be stored until needed. (Battleship *North Carolina*)

This *North Carolina* Kingfisher carries a January 1943-introduced tri-color camouflage scheme of Non-specular Sea Blue wing and stabilizer leading edges, semi-gloss Sea Blue on the balance of the wing and stabilizer upper surfaces, Non-specular Intermediate Blue on vertical surfaces, and Non-specular Insignia White on undersides. The floats had Non-specular White undersides and Non-specular Sea Blue upper surfaces. The OS2U-3 was armed with one flexible Browning .30-caliber machine gun in the radioman/observer's compartment and a fixed Browning .30-caliber machine gun in the starboard wing root. Each gun had 600 rounds of ammunition. The Kingfisher also could carry two 100-pound or 250-pound bombs or 325-pound depth charges.

Into Combat

Following the Japanese aerial attack on Pearl Harbor, the antiaircraft suite of *North Carolina* was augmented with additional light weapons. The ship, however, remained in waters off the Eastern U.S. as a deterrent against the German battleship *Tirpitz*.

That situation changed in July 1942, however, when *North Carolina* arrived in the Pacific. Although not yet fitted with the 40mm Bofors battery that would become prevalent in later years, *North Carolina's* antiaircraft were still among the most sophisticated and powerful in the fleet, and she was assigned to protect the fleet's aircraft carriers.

North Carolina first made contact with the enemy on the afternoon of 24 August 1942 as she was screening the USS *Enterprise*. The carrier came under attack by 36 Japanese dive bombers, which were escorted by numerous fighter aircraft. Weeks of intense training on the part of *North Carolina's* crew paid off as she hurled rounds upward to protect the carrier.

When the Japanese attackers' attention turned to *North Carolina*, the volume of antiaircraft gunfire, with its smoke and muzzle flashes, was such that Rear Admiral Thomas Kincaid, Commander Task Force 16, signaled from his flagship *Enterprise* the question "Are you afire?" Despite the ferocity of her barrage, *North Carolina* did not escape unscathed. Damage to the ship itself was inconsequential, but newlywed Aviation Machinist Mate 3rd Class George Conlon of New York – a loader on one of the aft 20mm guns – was hit by Japanese strafing and died before he could be treated. Conlon was the first of 10 *North Carolina* crew to die in the Pacific, an additional 64 would be wounded before the Japanese surrender.

The *North Carolina's* first combat was in the Battle of the Eastern Solomons on 24 August 1942. While she was guarding the carrier USS *Enterprise,* Japanese dive-bombers and torpedo-bombers attacked the carrier. The *North Carolina* filled the sky with antiaircraft fire, using all the AA guns it could bring to bear. A total of 841 5-inch rounds alone were fired. Some of those flak bursts are visible in this photo. (Battleship *North Carolina*)

A snapshot taken from the USS *North Carolina* during the Battle of the Eastern Solomons shows one of her seven near misses from Japanese bombs. One enlisted man was killed and the ship suffered slight damage from strafing during the engagement. (Battleship *North Carolina*)

Spent cartridge casings litter a deck on the USS *North Carolina* following the Battle of the Eastern Solomons. (Battleship *North Carolina*)

77

A crewman pitches a spent 5-inch cartridge casing next to the 5-inch loading machines after the Battle of the Eastern Solomons. (Battleship *North Carolina*)

Spent cartridge casings, such as these on the 03 level, would be collected and later recycled into new cartridge cases. (Battleship *North Carolina*)

One Japanese projectile from the strafing, .428 inches in diameter, was found embedded on the *North Carolina's* teak deck. (Battleship *North Carolina*)

Torpedo . . . headed for you!

North Carolina's closest scrape with disaster occurred while escorting the aircraft carrier USS *Wasp en route* to Guadalcanal on 15 September 1942. At 1445 hours (2:45 PM) *North Carolina's* officer of the deck, Lt (jg) Robert Celustka, noticed smoke rising from *Wasp.* In the absence of any signal from *Wasp,* he believed this to be the result of a minor aircraft accident, but noted that the fire seemed to be spreading. Suddenly, the radio came alive with garbled message including in part "…torpedo head for formation…". Signal flags fluttered from the destroyer *Mustin,* DD-413, warning of torpedoes. Another broken radio transmission came through "….torpedo just passed astern of me, headed for you!" Who the "you" was, however, was unclear.

At that moment, Seaman Second Class Albert S. Geary was blown off the deck and lost at sea. Below decks Ingwald Nelson was testing the air in void spaces while William Skelton and Oscar Stone were measuring oil in fuel tanks near the port bow, and Leonard Pone was showering in a nearby head. Who the "you" was became abundantly clear as the sea adjacent the port bow erupted into a cascade of salt water and fuel oil. Nelson, Skelton, and Stone were killed instantly, while Pone drowned, a result of being trapped by the sealing of watertight doors. Disaster was narrowly averted when burning oil from ruptured tanks crept across the deck of the turret-two projectile room. Quick thinking crewmembers activated the sprinklers, flooding the space and preventing a catastrophic magazine explosion, similar to the one that destroyed the *Arizona* at Pearl Harbor.

Her engineering plant unscathed, *North Carolina* picked up speed and held her position in the formation, despite the thousand tons of seawater that entered the hole opened by the torpedo. Counterflooding quickly trimmed the initial 5-degree list back to an even keel, and *North Carolina* headed to Pearl for repair – emerging 15 November even more heavily armed than before.

On 15 September 1942 the *North Carolina* was escorting Marine troop ships as part of the USS *Hornet* Task Force southeast of Guadalcanal, when Japanese submarines attacked their vessels and those of the neighboring USS *Wasp* Task Force. Japanese submarine I-19, shown here, fired a spread of torpedoes and scored hits on the aircraft carrier USS *Wasp* (CV-2), destroyer *O'Brien* (DD-415), and USS *North Carolina.* The I-19 was a Type B1 fleet submarine armed with six 533mm forward torpedo tubes and laden with 17 torpedoes. The torpedoes that wrought destruction to *Wasp,* damaged the *North Carolina,* and mortally wounded the *O'Brien* were the Type 92. (Battleship *North Carolina*)

USS *Wasp* in the foreground and USS *North Carolina* in the right distance steam ahead in a photograph probably taken on 15 September 1942, not long before both ships were struck by torpedoes from I-19. While *Wasp's* range from I-19 was about 200 yards, the *North Carolina* was some 12,000 yards from I-19. The torpedo that hit *North Carolina* passed under two destroyers first. (National Archives)

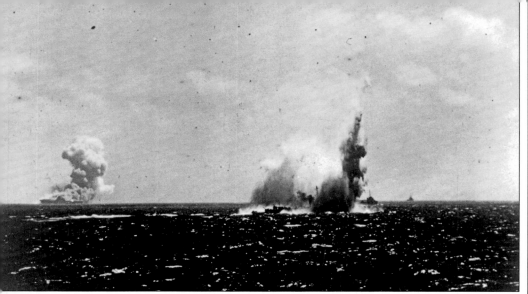

On 15 September, a Japanese torpedo strikes the USS *O'Brien* to the right as explosions and fires wrack the USS *Wasp* in the distance. Moments after the *O'Brien* was hit, at 14:52 a torpedo detonated on the forward port hull of USS *North Carolina*. Thus, in one torpedo spread, I-19 achieved the feat of sinking the *Wasp* and the *O'Brien* and seriously damaging *North Carolina*. (National Archives)

As viewed from astern, the *North Carolina* lists, smoke billowing out of her, shortly after the ship was torpedoed. The torpedo punctured the port side of the hull below the belt armor adjacent to turret one, flooding many of the compartments from the third deck down, causing a pronounced list to port. Cascading water from the torpedo explosion washed one man off the deck to his death. (National Archives)

Quick thinking, along with the USS *North Carolina's* design, allowed the crew to save the ship after a torpedo tore through her port bow. Although approximately one thousand tons of water poured into the forward port part of the hull, the ship's watertight compartments confined the flooding, and the crew stabilized the listing ship by counterflooding void tanks on the starboard side of the hull. Crewmen shored up watertight doors such as this one to prevent the massive pressure of the water from buckling them. This door was in the crew's washroom in compartment A310L, at frame 39. (Battleship *North Carolina*)

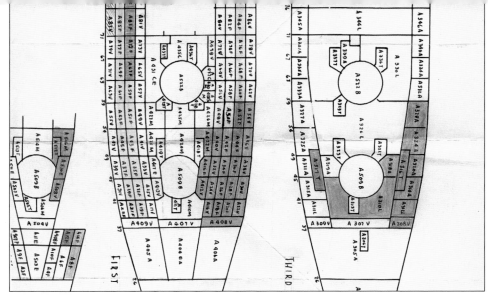

In a diagram filed with a report on the USS *North Carolina's* torpedo damages, the areas in red on the third deck and the first and second platforms indicate where water from the torpedo explosion flooded into compartments. Yellow signifies compartments already filled with fuel oil, while green and blue indicate, respectively, sea ballast and counterflooded compartments. (Battleship *North Carolina*)

The torpedo struck the ship to the port side of turret one, causing various damages to the belowdecks structure of the turret, including warping the deck plates of the inner circle of the powder-handling room, as seen here. Five members of the North Carolina's crew were killed in the attack and 23 wounded. Subsequently, the ship retired to Pearl Harbor for repairs. (Battleship *North Carolina*)

Whiplash from the torpedo explosion caused damage to the CXAM-1 search radar antenna high atop the foremast, including a bent frame, broken supports, and missing struts. The whiplash also caused the high-frequency transmission line of the CXAM-1 to break. These damages rendered the radar useless. (Battleship *North Carolina*)

The blast from the torpedo explosion caused multiple breaks in the supports for the CXAM-1 search radar. *North Carolina's* crew literally tied the array to the ship with hemp rope in order to prevent it from being lost overboard. Permanent repairs were made to the array when the ship reached Pearl Harbor.

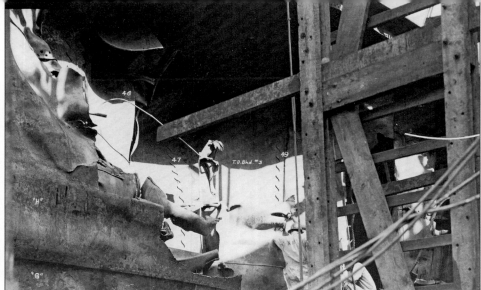

In drydock at Pearl Harbor, repairs are underway on the breach in the port side of the hull caused by the Japanese torpedo. The opening measured 32 feet long by 18 feet high. During a stop *en route* from the Solomons to Pearl Harbor, the ship briefly stopped in Tongatabu in the Friendly Islands, where divers cut off ripped plating protruding around the breach. (Battleship *North Carolina*)

This view taken on 11 October 1942 documents the breach on the port side of USS *North Carolina* from the outside of the hull facing aft. The ship had arrived at Pearl Harbor on 30 September but had to wait 10 days to enter drydock because the USS *South Dakota* was already in the only drydock at Pearl Harbor of a size sufficiently large to hold the *North Carolina*. (National Archives)

The forward end of the breach in the hull of USS *North Carolina* is viewed from outside on 11 October 1942, the day after the ship entered drydock. There are scaffolding legs and planks on the outside of the hull. The torpedo struck the hull between frames 45 and 46, some 12 feet below the waterline and 2 feet below the bottom of the battleship's belt armor. (National Archives)

The torpedo explosion cracked the *North Carolina's* belt armor in several places. One crack ran diagonally between frames 42 and 43. One of the additional cracks is shown here, visible at the vertex of the angle mounting bar, which itself is torn and pulled from its rivets. The cracks were not deemed severe enough to require immediate repairs, and would remain until her refit at Puget Sound in late 1944. (Battleship *North Carolina*)

Workmen assess the damages in this view from below and forward of the torpedo breach taken on 11 October 1942. The location of frame 45 is indicated below the scaffold beam. The locations of strakes G and H are also marked on the photo. A strake is a longitudinal course of plating of the shell, or outer skin, of the hull. Extensive rippling is visible on the strakes. (Battleship *North Carolina*)

On 8 November 1942, repairs are completed on the torpedo breach in the hull of USS *North Carolina* in drydock at Pearl Harbor. The ship was being repainted in a new camouflage scheme: Measure 21, Navy Blue System, which consisted of Navy Blue (5-N) on all vertical surfaces and Deck Blue (20-B) on the decks. An area amidships on the hull has yet to be painted. (Battleship *North Carolina*)

The USS *North Carolina* acquired its first Bofors 40mm antiaircraft guns while undergoing repairs at Pearl Harbor in October and November 1942, replacing the 1.1-inch guns and .50-caliber machine guns. In this 15 November 1942 photograph, the quad 40mm mount on the port side of the top of the pilot house and chart house is shown. A similar mount was on the starboard side. These mounts were on each side of the forward fire-control tower, visible to the right. Another 40mm gun mount within a tub-type splinter shield is on a lower deck, in the background. In the tub toward the top center is a Mk. 51 director, with which an operator could acquire and track targets with the unit's Mk. 14 gyro lead-computing gun sight and control an adjacent 40mm gun mount. (Battleship *North Carolina*)

Several new features introduced during the repairs and refitting at Pearl Harbor in October and November 1942 are visible in this view taken on 15 November 1942. In the foreground is a 40mm quad antiaircraft gun mount within a tub-type armored splinter shield, located on port side of the aft superstructure two levels above the superstructure deck, with a tub for a Mk. 51 director above and forward of it. A similar mount with splinter shield was on the starboard side of the same level. Above and aft of the 40mm mount is the aft Mk. 37 secondary-battery director, which finally had been fitted with a Mk. 4 radar antenna on an extended frame. To the far left is the kingpost of the port boat crane, while just aft of it is the Mk. 38 main battery director. To the lower right is turret three. (Battleship *North Carolina*)

Also photographed at Pearl Harbor on 15 November 1942 was a 40mm antiaircraft gun mount and splinter shield on the port side of the superstructure deck between frames 74 and 76. A similar 40mm mount was on the opposite side of the superstructure deck, with both mounts being situated near the forward part of the superstructure. Aft of the mount is 5-inch mount number two. (Battleship *North Carolina*)

The 40mm antiaircraft gun mount in the preceding photograph is viewed from above. An opening in the splinter shield allowed crewmen access to the mount. Around the inner sides of the splinter shield are racks for the four-round clips of 40mm ammunition that loaders would manually feed into the tops of the receivers of the guns. The platform and guard rail for the loaders are visible. (Battleship *North Carolina*)

During the October-November 1942 refit and repairs at Pearl Harbor, two 40mm gun mounts with splinter shields were installed on the fantail on each side of the aircraft-handling crane. These mounts replaced four 20mm guns that had been located in that area. Inboard of each 40mm mount is a tub-type splinter shield with a Mk. 51 director protruding above the top. (Naval History and Heritage Command)

The starboard 40mm gun mount on the fantail is viewed in this 15 November 1942 photograph. The four 40mm guns are elevated within the tub-type splinter shield. Rising above the forward part of the splinter shield is a Mk. 51 director, with its tub partially visible. A clear view is also offered of the aircraft-handling crane between the 40mm gun mounts. (National Archives)

This overall view of the USS *North Carolina* from off the port stern was taken one day after the preceding series of photographs, on 16 November 1942, shows the ship nearly ready to return to the war. From this angle, visible features that had been installed during the ship's October-November 1942 stay in Pearl Harbor include the two 40mm gun mounts on the fantail and the Mk. 4 radar antenna atop the aft Mk. 37 secondary-battery director, on an elevated frame to preserve the line of sight of the Mk. 38 director. Quad 40mm gun mounts are also now present on the main deck on each side of the aft superstructure, as a close examination of this photo reveals. The new suite of quad 40mm guns the *North Carolina* acquired in the fall of 1942 gave the battleship a far greater medium- and close-range defensive capability against attacking aircraft than had the 1.1-inch guns. (National Archives)

The USS *North Carolina* presents her stern to the photographer on 16 November 1942. The prominent new 40mm gun tubs on the fantail remain fixtures on the ship to this day. The new camouflage scheme of Measure 21, Navy Blue System, gave the ship an overall darker tone than her previous schemes. In this scheme, the ship's name was not painted on the stern. However, the ship's number, 55, is painted in a lighter color on the hull, forward of the 40mm gun tubs. (National Archives)

The bow of the USS *North Carolina* is emphasized in this 16 November 1942 view taken at Pearl Harbor. The 5-inch gun mounts are elevated and trained outward. The newly repaired CXAM-1 search radar antenna on the foremast towers above the rest of the ship. Protruding from both sides of the superstructure aft of the pilot house are the tubs of the two new 40mm gun mounts. This protruding arrangement would give these mounts an excellent field of fire to the front. (National Archives)

Freshly repainted and now boasting a revamped antiaircraft artillery suite, the USS *North Carolina* was now ready to reenter the fight in November 1942. With her 40 new 40mm guns in 10 quad mounts, the ship would be much better adapted to combat the increasingly ferocious Japanese air assaults on U.S. naval forces in the Pacific. The day after this 16 November photograph was taken, the ship departed Pearl Harbor, bound once again for the South Pacific. First, the *North Carolina* would sail off Oahu for two days, engaging in live-firing exercises before proceeding to the Solomons area to join the *Enterprise* Task Force. (National Archives)

USS *North Carolina* is underway at sea after her October-November 1942 repairs and refitting at Pearl Harbor. She exhibits her new quad 40mm antiaircraft mounts. In addition to those guns, changes had been made to the ship's lighter antiaircraft guns. The .50-caliber machine guns had been eliminated, and additional 20mm guns were installed. On the foredeck aft of the forecastle, splinter shields now enclosed four 20mm guns on each side of the deck instead of the previous two per side. Other revisions to the 20mm antiaircraft gun suite included a new, three-gun suite within a common splinter shield on the main deck on each side of the forward part of the superstructure, from about frames 70 to 77. (National Archives)

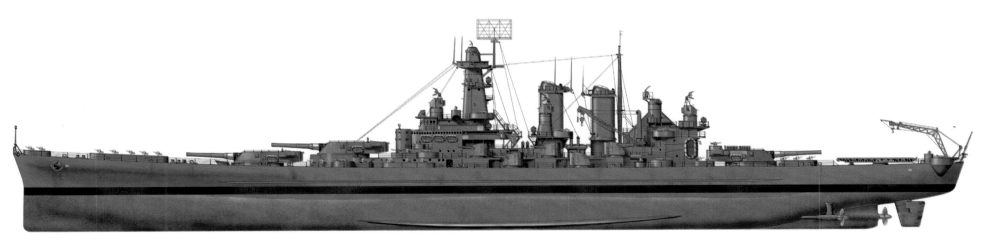

Concurrent to repair of torpedo damage in November 1942, *North Carolina* was repainted into a Measure 21 camouflage scheme consisting of 5-N Navy Blue on all vertical surfaces and 20-B Deck Blue on all decks. *North Carolina* wore this scheme until September 1943.

A view from the forecastle of the *North Carolina* following the October-November 1942 refitting provides a glimpse of the new 20mm antiaircraft gun positions on the starboard side of the foredeck. Three of the guns are visible, and one more is out of view aft of those guns. In the foreground is a 20mm ready-ammunition locker, protected on the sides with armor plates. (Battleship *North Carolina*)

Crewmembers of the 40mm gun mount on the forward starboard side of the superstructure deck enjoy a few moments of relaxation. Some four-round ammunition clips are stored on the inside of the splinter shield. In the right background is turret two, trained to starboard, and to the bottom left, on the main deck, is a 20mm gun, one of three recently installed in that area of the deck. (Battleship *North Carolina*)

Personnel of the 5-inch/38-caliber secondary battery conduct loading drills using the two loading machines, practice equipment for improving the gun crews' proficiency, on the port side of the superstructure deck aft of the number-two 5-inch turret, which is visible at the top. The 5-inch ammunition was semi-fixed, consisting of the projectile and a brass cartridge with powder charge. (Battleship *North Carolina*)

A paravane, a towed, submersible anti-mine device, is rigged on a paravane boom. When lowered into the water, the paravane would swing out away from the ship, go underwater, and detonate any submerged mines encountered, or sever their anchoring cables so gunners on the ship could detonate the mine. The *North Carolina* carried several of these. (Battleship *North Carolina*)

Famed photographer Edward Steichen, or a member of his U.S. Navy photographic team, took this color photo of the *North Carolina* during the Gilbert Islands campaign in November 1943. The ship is painted in a Measure 32/18D camouflage scheme, which probably had been applied within the preceding two months. Recent research indicates that the darkest color in the scheme was Dull Black (BK), with the next darker shade on the horizontal surfaces being Ocean Gray (5-O) and the lightest shade being Light Gray (5-L). A prominent new feature was the platform with splinter shield partway up the forward fire-control tower, intended to provide Batt Two, the executive officer's (XO) battle station, with better visibility. (Stan Piet Collection)

As is apparent in this aerial photo of the USS *North Carolina* taken on 12 November 1943, under this ship's Measure 32/18D camouflage scheme, the decks and horizontal surfaces were painted in patterns of Deck Blue (20-B), Ocean Gray, and Dull Black. The demarcations between the different colors were applied roughly, largely in curved or squiggly patterns rather than in straight lines. The ship had left Pearl Harbor two days earlier, and a week after this photo was taken, she would participate in the bombardment of Makin Island in the Gilberts. The new platform surrounding the forward fire-control tower is visible. It was nicknamed Stryker's Bridge after the ship's XO, Commander Joe W. Stryker, who ordered the construction of the platform. (National Archives)

An aircraft from USS *Essex* (CV-9) photographed the *North Carolina* as she sailed for the Marianas with Task Force 58.3 in June 1944. Compared with the preceding two photos, the camouflage paint appears to have faded considerably under the tropical sun in the intervening seven months, with the Dull Black appearing almost a dark gray. (National Archives)

In September 1943 North Carolina was repainted in theater in a dazzle camouflage scheme designated Measure 32/18D. The colors utilized were dull black, 5-O Ocean Gray and 5-L Light Gray. Because this was field applied, the demarcation between colors was not as crisp as specified, and there was a small black patch on the starboard bow – an area that by specification should have been Ocean Gray.

Somewhere in the Pacific, crewmen of the *North Carolina* enjoy a swim alongside the port forward side of the ship, making full recreational use of torpedo-net buoys rigged around the ship. The patterns of the three colors applied to the horizontal surfaces in the first version of the Measure 32/18D camouflage scheme are apparent, as is the crude demarcation between colors. (Battleship *North Carolina*)

An aerial photograph of the USS *North Carolina* taken sometime between September 1943 and September 1944 depicts the first version of the Measure 32/18D camouflage. Although the main and superstructure decks appear to have been stripped of their camouflage paint, this seems to be an illusion occasioned by an overexposed photo. (Battleship *North Carolina*)

A view of the *North Carolina* anchored offshore somewhere in the Pacific reveals some details of the patterns of the first version of the Measure 32/18D camouflage scheme on the forward decks, superstructure, and gun mounts. Ocean Gray predominates on the port and center parts of the foredeck, while on the starboard side are a very faded Dull Black and Deck Blue, the slightly lighter color. Arrayed underwater around the ship and supported by numerous buoys is a torpedo net, designed to absorb the kinetic energy of a torpedo and defeat it. Booms hold the net at a predetermined distance from the ship. Canvas awnings are erected at points over the main deck; the ones aft of turret two are stained a dark color. (Battleship *North Carolina*)

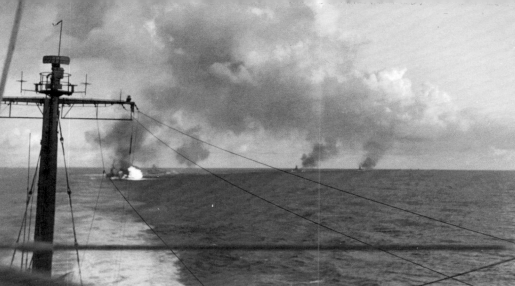

An 8 December 1943 photograph taken on USS *North Carolina* shows the first salvo from the ship striking the Japanese airfield on the southern coast Nauru, an island some 400 miles southwest of Tarawa. The *North Carolina* fired the first salvo prematurely, enabling the crew to claim the honor of firing the first 16-inch salvo of the war against a Japanese shore target. (Battleship *North Carolina*)

In this chart of the results of the bombardment of Nauru, small circles with numbers represent designated targets, and the square and rectangular boxes with dotted lines represent the fall of projectiles as reported by a spotting plane. The airfield is along the coast near the bottom of the map; directly above it is a radar installation that came under a heavy concentration of fire. (Battleship *North Carolina*)

To the right of the *North Carolina's* mainmast, USS *Indiana* (BB-58) unleashes a 16-inch salvo on the Japanese airfield on Nauru. Powder smoke from other ships farther away in the line appears in the distance. Other battleships involved in the operation were the *Alabama* (BB-60), *Massachusetts* (BB-59), *South Dakota* (BB-57), and Washington. (Battleship *North Carolina*)

The bombardment of Nauru completed, large plumes of smoke tower over the island as the attacking force retires. At the bottom, personnel in the forward Mk. 37 secondary-battery director observe the effects of the barrage on the island. A good view is offered of the Mk. 4 fire-control radar antenna and its mounting frame on top of the director. (Battleship *North Carolina*)

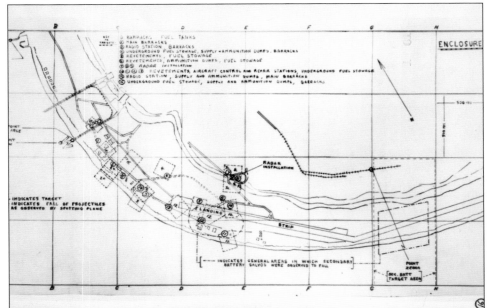

A photo dated January 1944 documents a Mk. 3 Mod. 2 radar antenna on a pedestal mount projecting from the front of the forward fire-control tower, above Stryker's bridge. Formerly, this antenna had been mounted on top of the forward Mk. 38 main-battery director, but it was moved to the new position after a new Mk. 8 radar antenna was installed over the Mk. 38 director. (National Archives)

A close-up view shows the aft part of the SC pedestal mount for the Mk. 3 Mod. 2 radar antenna on the front face of the forward fire-control tower in January 1944. Later that year, the antenna was dismounted. In the background the faint lines of the bow of the ship are visible, as are a series of torpedo-net buoys surrounding the ship. (National Archives)

USS *North Carolina,* left, and her sister ship, USS *Washington,* advance across the Pacific on 24 January 1944, *en route* to support the U.S. invasion of Kwajalein Atoll in the Marshall Islands. While the *North Carolina* is still in the first version of her Measure 32/18D camouflage, the *Washington* sports the Measure 22 pattern that it had had since September 1942. (Naval History and Heritage Command)

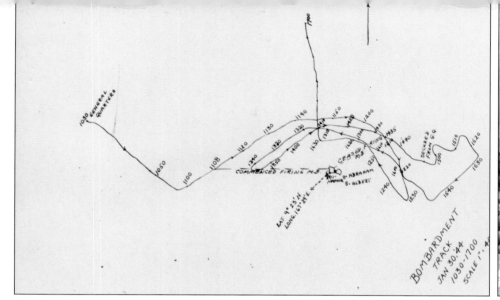

On January 29-30, 1944, the *North Carolina* participated in the bombardment of Japanese fortifications on the adjoining islands of Roi-Namur in Kwajalein Atoll, Marshall Islands. This chart shows the bombardment track of the ship, commencing with general quarters at 1030 to the west of the islands, until the conclusion at 1700 hours, to the north of the islands. (Battleship *North Carolina*)

In a photograph dated 3 February 1944, nothing but debris and the twisted frame remains of a Japanese hangar on Roi. The barrage also destroyed Japanese barracks, pillboxes and other fortifications, and ammunition dumps. The capture of Roi-Namur, in which the *North Carolina* played a key role, was an important achievement in the U.S. island-hopping campaign. (Battleship *North Carolina*)

U.S. Marine Corps invasion forces found this scene of destruction on Roi Island on 2 February 1944 following the *North Carolina's* bombardment of the Japanese base. It had once been the site of a key Japanese airfield. Together with a U.S. air assault on Roi-Namur on 29 January, the USS *North Carolina's* bombardment negated any chance of Japanese air superiority in the battle. (Battleship *North Carolina*)

In addition to bombarding the island, the *North Carolina* scored a kill on a Japanese freighter, *Eiko Maru,* that was sighted inside the lagoon south of Roi-Namur. In this photo taken from a spotting plane, shells explode around the beleaguered freighter. Later, the Navy made an intelligence coup by salvaging from *Eiko Maru* secret charts of various Japanese bases. (National Archives)

USS *North Carolina* accompanied a fast carrier strike force in an assault on the important Japanese naval base at Truk Atoll on 16-17 February 1944. The U.S. forces destroyed or put out of commission 39 Japanese ships and over 300 aircraft. The *North Carolina* would return to Truk in April 1944. Here, a Douglas Dauntless dive-bomber flies over Truk Atoll in April 1944. (National Archives)

On 29-30 April 1944, U.S. naval aircraft assault Japanese shipping off Dublon Island, Truk Atoll. On 30 April, Lt. John A. Burns, pilot of a *North Carolina* OS2U Kingfisher, performed an act of heroism by landing his floatplane in rough seas, rescuing 10 downed naval aviators, and taxiing with the fliers on the wings to the submarine USS *Tang,* which took them aboard. (National Archives)

On 29 or 30 April 1944, U.S. Navy aircraft assault Dublon Island, Truk Atoll. To the left, smoke rises from Japanese shipping and the naval base on the island. The USS *North Carolina* was in the vicinity during the attack, and at first light on the 30th two OS2U Kingfishers from the ship, piloted by Lts. j.g. John A. Burns and J.J. Dowdle launched to search for downed pilots. (Battleship *North Carolina*)

In April 1944 the USS *North Carolina* joined the USS *Enterprise* group to provide fire support during the U.S. landings at Hollandia, New Guinea. The attacks commenced on the 21st, and this photo was taken while the naval force continued the bombardment the following day. In the foreground, amphibious vehicles proceed toward shore, while bombarding ships are in the background. (Naval Historical Foundation)

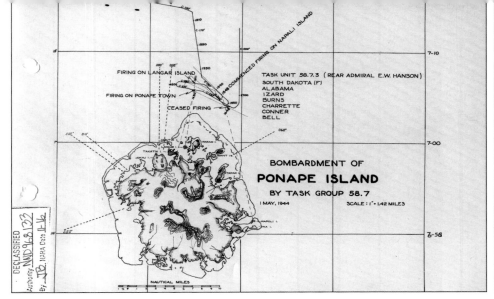

The *North Carolina,* along with six other fast battleships, participated in the bombardment of Japanese targets on Ponape Island in the Caroline Islands on 1 May 1944. The island had a harbor, an airfield, another airfield under construction, and a seaplane base. This chart indicates the track of part of the force that bombarded the island. (Battleship *North Carolina*)

Although this photograph of the USS *North Carolina* has been published in several books with captions stating that it was taken during the Gilbert Islands Campaign in September 1943, the crewman who reportedly took the photo claims it was taken off Saipan in the Marianas Islands on 13 June 1944, the first day of the naval bombardment of the west side of that island. (Battleship *North Carolina*)

This chart attached to USS *North Carolina's* official report of the bombardment of the western shore of Saipan tracks the course of the ship on 13 June 1944. The solid lines with arrows mark the ship's courses, while the interrupted lines indicate the direction of the ship's 16-inch salvoes. Grid coordinates for directing fire are marked on the land portion of the map to the lower right. (Battleship *North Carolina*)

The naval bombardment of Saipan from 13 to 15 June followed air strikes on that island and nearby Tinian on 11-13 June. On 15 June, a Marine landing force invaded Saipan. That night, the *North Carolina* shot down an enemy aircraft. Capturing these two islands provided U.S. forces with suitable locations for B-29 bomber bases, which would prove crucial in winning the war. (Battleship *North Carolina*)

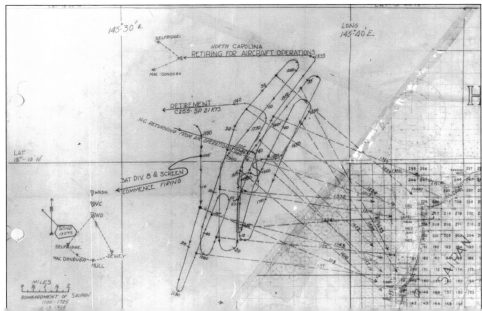

The USS *North Carolina* makes a sharp change of course off Saipan, visible in the background, on 13 June 1944, providing cover for minesweeping operations preparatory to the U.S. landings. During an 85-minute span, the ship pounded targets ashore at average ranges of about 15,000 yards. During the engagement, the *North Carolina* fired 360 16-inch rounds and 2,096 5-inch rounds. (Battleship *North Carolina*)

This chart tracks the *North Carolina's* track from 0900 hours to 1830 on 19 June 1944, including notations of one Jill and one Kate "splashed" by the ship. Although Task Force 58 proceeded west to attempt to meet the Japanese fleet, 19 June developed into a massive air battle that became known as the Marianas Turkey Shoot, in which the Japanese lost most of their planes. (Battleship *North Carolina*)

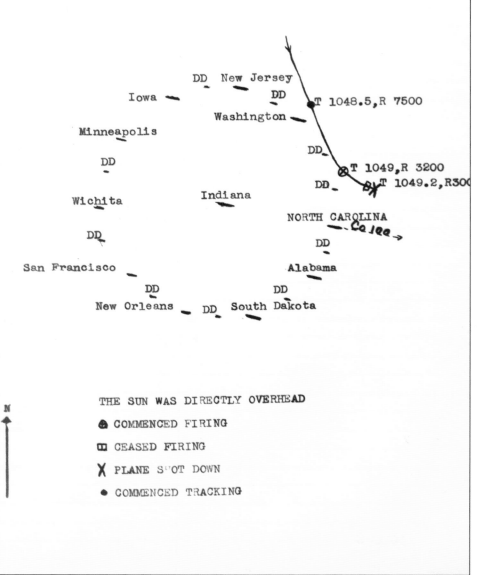

The Japanese mounted a massive aerial attack on Task Force 58 some 130 miles southwest of Saipan on 19 and 20 June 1944; it would become known as the Battle of the Philippine Sea. This chart shows Task Force 58's Task Group 58.7, which included the *North Carolina,* in an air-defense formation. The hand-written X to the right indicates a downed Japanese aircraft. (Battleship *North Carolina*)

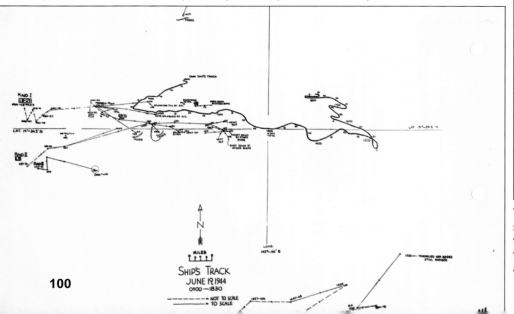

Following a refitting at Puget Sound Navy Yard, Bremerton, Washington, USS *North Carolina* shows off her new, second version of her Measure 32/18D camouflage scheme on 23 September 1944. This version featured a much neater, straighter application of the demarcations between the colors, which included Light Gray, Ocean Gray, and Dull Black on vertical surfaces. Horizontal surfaces, including decks, were Deck Blue, with the exception of the top of turret three, which was Ocean Gray. Another key identifying feature introduced in this refitting was the round SK-2 search radar antenna atop the foremast, which replaced the rectangular CXAM-1 antenna. (Puget Sound Naval Shipyard)

A Break in the Action

Years of operating in forward areas took their toll on both *North Carolina* and her men, and finally in early July 1944 she was detached from Task Force 58 and began a 6,000-mile voyage to Puget Sound. Arriving on the last day of July, it was the first time in two years that the ship and her crew had been to the U.S. mainland. While the *North Carolina* received much-needed repairs and updating, the crew enjoyed a welcome respite from the rigors of combat. Personnel were divided into two groups, and alternately each was granted 25 days leave. Many took this opportunity to cement long-distance relationships, with several crewmen getting married before *North Carolina's* 25 September departure, bound once again for enemy waters.

When *North Carolina* left Bremerton, the Measure 32/18D camouflage finish covering her outer surfaces had been freshly reapplied by the yard force at Puget Sound. Much of her interior had been repainted as well, by both ship's company and the yard force. Belt armor plates numbers 3, 4, and 5 were removed, structural repairs made to the shell, and new armor plates furnished by the Bureau of Ships were installed, using 120 new armor bolts. While in the yard the aircraft handling crane was reinforced, and all-new foremast and mainmasts were manufactured and installed. The sky control platform was enlarged some 16 inches, and even more significantly, new search radars were installed and a new Combat Information Center was created on the flag bridge level.

One of USS *North Carolina's* high-pressure turbines was photographed in August 1944 during a refitting at Puget Sound Navy Yard. Steam from the boilers drove four sets of turbines, which drove the propeller shafts. Each turbine had a 12-stage high-pressure impulse, 6-stage low-pressure impulse, and 3-stage astern impulse. (Battleship *North Carolina*)

A low-pressure turbine is displayed with its casing raised for inspection in August 1944. The sailor to the far left provides a sense of the turbine's scale. During the ship's July-September 1944 refitting at Puget Sound, the main turbines were thoroughly inspected, clearances were gauged, and oil seals, bearings, packings, and couplings were serviced. (Battleship *North Carolina*)

In a 25 September 1944 photo, the new dish-shaped SK-2 air-search antenna is on the foremast to the left. Mark 8 fire-control radars replaced the Mk. 3 radars on top of the Mk. 38 main-battery directors. The mount for the Mk. 4 radar atop the aft Mk. 37 director was lowered, and a Mk. 22 "orange-peel" radar antenna was mounted on its starboard side. (NARA Seattle via Tracy White)

A new mainmast and new foremast were installed during the 31 July-25 September 1944 refitting, and on the rear of the mainmast is a new feature: a ventilation system for the mast's cabling. The Mk. 8 radar antenna atop the Mk. 38 director is under wraps. Below the director is a 40mm gun mount; these quad gun mounts previously had received armored shields on their fronts and sides. The port boat crane is also shown in detail. (NARA Seattle via Tracy White)

The new Mk. 22 orange-peel radar antenna is prominent on the side of the Mk. 4 radar on the forward Mk. 37 secondary-battery director. The Sky Control platform on the upper part of the forward fire-control tower was enlarged during this refitting. Below Sky Control, the Mk. 3 antenna had been removed. Above Sky Control on the Mk. 38 director, the new Mk. 8 radar is under cover. A new yardarm was installed on the foremast. (NARA Seattle via Tracy White)

A broadside view of the *North Carolina* at Puget Sound Navy Yard on 24 September 1944, the day before her departure, showcases the ship's new, late-version Measure 32/18D camouflage scheme as it appeared on her starboard side. Straight lines and precisely defined angles now replaced the meandering lines and curves of the previous first-version Measure 32/18D scheme. (Puget Sound Naval Shipyard)

On 26 September 1944 the USS *North Carolina* is underway, making 26 knots, in Puget Sound, Washington, following her two-month-long refitting. That refitting had included a schedule of hundreds, if not thousands, of maintenance procedures and modifications: everything from a revamping of the ship's ice cream-making equipment to installation of a new combat information center. (Puget Sound Naval Shipyard)

During the July-September 1944 refit at Puget Sound, four new 20mm mounts were added to the forecastle and foredeck at frames 1½ and 17, along with protected-type ready-service ammunition boxes. Thus, as seen here, there were now four 20mm mounts on the forecastle, two on each side, with an elongated C-shaped splinter shield protecting each fore-and-aft pair of gun mounts. (Puget Sound Naval Shipyard)

The *North Carolina* is viewed from astern at Puget Sound Navy Yard, Bremerton, Washington, on 24 September 1944. A motorized boat is moored to the boat boom extended alongside the quarterdeck. The black cover has been removed from the Mk. 8 radar antenna mounted over the aft Mk. 38 main-battery director. The new, lower mount for the aft Mk. 37 director's Mk. 4 radar antenna is also noticeable. (Puget Sound Naval Shipyard)

On 26 September 1944 the *North Carolina* plows through Puget Sound at 26 knots. The ship's maximum rated speed was 28 knots at 199 rpm. The *North Carolina's* Vought Kingfishers are once again mounted on the catapults. During the refitting and overhaul at Puget Sound Navy Yard, the ship's crew enjoyed a 25-day leave in two groups, with half of the crew remaining with the ship while the other half enjoyed their time ashore. Now, the crew and their ship were ready to reenter the fray. Following a stop at Pearl Harbor in late October, the ship would sail to the U.S. Navy's advanced base at Ulithi Atoll in the western Caroline Islands before participating in operations in support of the campaign to retake the Philippines. (Puget Sound Naval Shipyard)

In September 1944 *North Carolina* was repainted once again following her refit at Puget Sound. While still in Measure 32/18D as she had been previously, there was a slight variation in the pattern, and as it was shipyard applied, the finish was much neater than it had been previously. The camouflage pattern did not extend onto her decks with this pattern, as it had with the earlier Theater-applied version. Instead, the decks were painted 20-B Deck Blue.

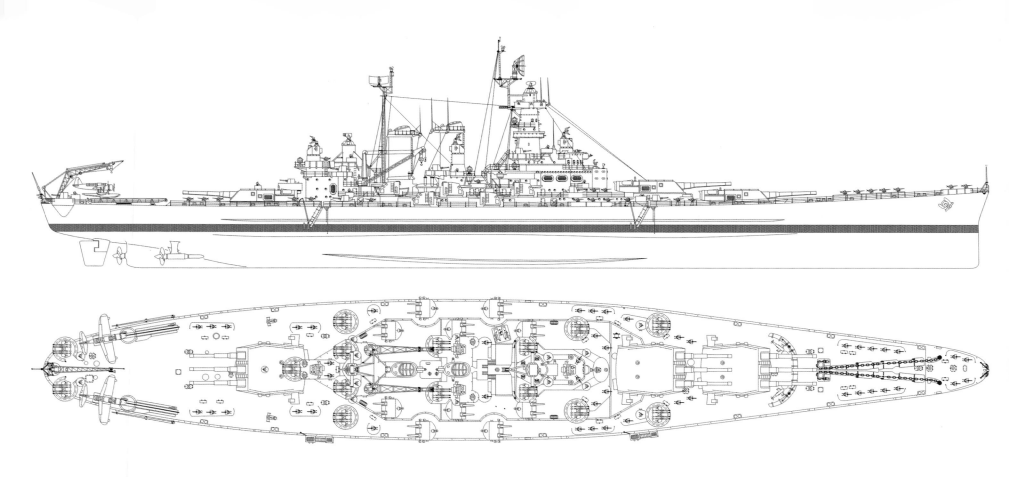

Antiaircraft Armament:	Heavy Machine Gun Battery:	sixty 40mm, arranged in 15 quadruple Mark 2 mounts.
	Medium Machine Gun Battery:	forty-eight 20mm Mount, Mark 4, single - with four 20mm mounts (two at frame 1½ and two at frame 17) added at Puget Sound during overhaul, April-September 1944.

Gun Directors:	Main Battery:	two Mark 38
	Secondary Battery:	four Mark 37
	40mm Battery:	fifteen Mark 51, Mod 1

Radar:	Search Radar:	SK-2
	Main Battery Fire Control Radar:	two Mk 8 Mod 2
	Secondary Battery Fire Control Radar:	four Mk 4 with Mk 22

For the United States Navy, at-sea refueling was a frequent and essential operation in the vast stretches of the Pacific Ocean. Here, the USS *North Carolina* performs an underway refueling from the oiler USS *Neches* (AO-47) on 30 November 1944. The photo was taken from the escort carrier USS *Sargent Bay* (CVL-83) as she approached the port beam of the *Neches* to refuel. (Battleship *North Carolina*)

Moments after the preceding photo was taken, the *Sargent Bay* approaches closer to the *Neches,* providing a close-up view of the *North Carolina* two months after her overhaul at Puget Sound Navy Yard. The new Mk. 8 radar over the aft Mk. 38 director is still under cover. Two of the batteship's Kingfishers, numbered 7 and 8, are parked on dollies on the fantail. (Puget Sound Naval Shipyard)

Waves crash between the *Neches,* in the foreground, and the *North Carolina* as the latter ship takes on fuel from the oiler. Visible on top of the conning tower of the *North Carolina* is a box-shaped housing that provided a base for a Mk. 27 radar antenna, a standby unit that replaced the Mk. 3 standby radar antenna formerly on front of the forward fire-control tower. (Battleship *North Carolina*)

As the *Sargent Bay* comes alongside the *Neches,* the *North Carolina* continues to take on fuel in the background. As a point of interest, the *Neches* was launched and commissioned in 1941 and operated extensively in the far reaches of the Pacific. She reportedly was the first oiler to enter Tokyo Bay at the conclusion of the war, and she went on to serve in the Vietnam War. (Battleship *North Carolina*)

On 25 November 1944, during operations off Luzon in the Philippines, a photographer on the North Carolina snapped this photo of the USS Essex (CV-9), prominent on the horizon, as a Japanese kamikaze plane was making a suicide dive at the carrier. In the foreground is one of the North Carolina's 36-inch searchlights. Five-inch mounts are poised for antiaircraft action. (National Archives)

A ball of fire rises over the USS Essex as the kamikaze crashes into the port side of her flight deck, detonating fueled aircraft on the deck. The carrier suffered considerable damage, and 15 crewmen were killed and 44 wounded. Nevertheless, the Essex was rapidly repaired and returned to action, serving through the rest of the war and beyond. (National Archives)

Following the kamikaze strike on the USS Essex, the carrier continues to smoke as her crew fights to extinguish fires and save the ship. Meantime, a few aircraft circle overhead while flak bursts pepper the sky. The destroyers, cruisers, and battleships strove to protect the aircraft carriers, but determined enemy aviators occasionally broke through the screen. (National Archives)

The North Carolina rests at an anchorage in the Pacific in November 1944. Two months after the ship left Puget Sound Navy Yard with a fresh camouflage paint job, the ship shows signs of extensive paint touchups on the hull. Crews strived to scrape and repaint peeling paint and corroded areas, as these were constants for a ship at sea. (Battleship North Carolina)

On 18 December 1944, as the *North Carolina* was operating with Task Force 38 in the Philippine Sea, a typhoon unexpectedly slammed into the force. *North Carolina* is seen contending with huge swells occasioned by the typhoon. Sources differ whether this photo of the *North Carolina* was taken before or after the typhoon struck. (National Archives)

The bow of the *North Carolina* takes a tremendous battering from the effects of the December 1944 typhoon. Personnel were cleared from the foredeck to avoid the loss of men overboard. Fortunately, no personnel were lost in the storm. Such was not the case throughout the task force: three destroyers sank, with the loss of some 800 crewmen. (Battleship *North Carolina*)

The forward end of the *North Carolina* disappears below the surface in a trough occasioned by the typhoon. Several members of the ship's crew later recounted that the typhoon was the fiercest storm and the most frightening episode of their lives. Several crewmen were almost swept off the deck at the height of the storm, saved only by lifelines. (Battleship *North Carolina*)

The bow of the *North Carolina* appears to be barely above water in a photo taken from the USS *Essex* either before or after the typhoon struck Task Force 38. During the height of the typhoon, troughs were encountered several hundred feet deep, with crests almost 1,000 feet apart. At times, the *North Carolina* rolled as much as 43 degrees to the side. (National Archives)

In a photo taken from USS *Ticonderoga* (CV-14) while supporting U.S. Navy carrier operations off the coast of French Indochina (now Vietnam) on 24 December 1944, USS *Washington* is next in line, followed by USS *North Carolina* and USS *South Dakota*. (National Archives)

Crewmen of USS *North Carolina's* refueling detail heave on lines as the ship prepares to refuel the destroyer coming alongside to the right. Although a battleship needed to refuel at sea, since the battleship had a very large fuel capacity, part of her duties was to refuel destroyers: a procedure the battleship carried out every few days during World War II. (Battleship *North Carolina*)

A refueling detail is at work during a refueling operation on the USS *North Carolina* around 1944, manipulating a line passing through a block secured to the deck. To the left is the rear of the gun house of a 5-inch gun mount, showing the aft port door open, providing a sense of the thickness of the door and the shield of the gun mount. Above the door is a rain gutter in the shape of an inverted V, a feature often found over doors on this ship. (Battleship *North Carolina*)

Receiving mail from home as well as sending mail to friends and relatives back in the States was a process essential for the morale of the crew. Here, mail is being transferred from an escort ship to the USS *North Carolina* in January 1945. (Battleship *North Carolina*)

Mail is being handed out on board the USS *North Carolina*. To maintain military secrecy, censors on the ship would remove any text in crewmen's letters that might compromise the security of the ship, including the ship's location, mission, or destination. (Battleship *North Carolina*)

Crewmen on the *North Carolina* wearing their skivvies, or underwear, sort mail below decks. Except for a few compartments, the interior of the ship was not air conditioned and could get extremely hot; wearing skivvies when appropriate was one way to cope with heat. The crewman on the left has written his name, Leppard, in ink on the waist band of his shorts, to identify them for washing purposes. (Battleship *North Carolina*)

113

The U.S. Marine Corps was tasked with invading the volcanic island of Iwo Jima, shown here, in February 1945, to secure for the U.S. Army Air Forces an advanced air base. The *North Carolina* participated in the pre-landing naval bombardment of the island. (Battleship *North Carolina*)

The invasion force is arrayed for battle on D-day on Iwo Jima, 19 February 1945, with transport ships standing by well offshore and landing craft advancing toward the shores. The *North Carolina's* assigned sector was to the right of the photo. (Battleship *North Carolina*)

Landing craft pass by a cordon of offshore bombardment craft, including to the right a battleship (possibly USS *Tennessee* BB-43) and smaller warships, on D-day at Iwo Jima. By the afternoon of D-day, nine battleships were offshore on the firing line. (Battleship *North Carolina*)

Smoke rises from Iwo Jima during a bombardment, Mount Suribachi in the foreground. The *North Carolina* remained off Iwo Jima until 22 February, providing fire support, including fire-on-call missions against specific targets identified by Marines on shore. (Battleship *North Carolina*)

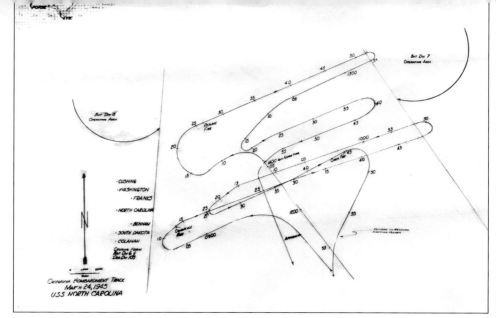

For the final major invasion of the war in the Pacific, the *North Carolina* participated in the pre-landing bombardment of Okinawa. This chart shows the ship's bombardment track on 24 March, when she shelled the southern end of the island. (Battleship *North Carolina*)

The USS *North Carolina* fires a salvo during the 24 March 1945 bombardment of Okinawa. The ship was part of a bombardment force that included seven other fast battleships. That day's bombardment was carried out at very long ranges. (Battleship *North Carolina*)

A salvo lands on map grid 8361N. The *North Carolina's* first targets on 24 March were a pillbox and an artillery position. One of the ship's Vought OS2U pilots, Lt. Almon P. Oliver, flew a spotting mission, correcting the fire and identifying new targets. (Battleship *North Carolina*)

On 24 March, Lieutenant Oliver discovered an "antique fort" and directed the ship's fire onto it, causing some damage to it. The fort turned out to be Shuri Castle, the major command center for the Japanese and, later, the site of a major ground battle. (Battleship *North Carolina*)

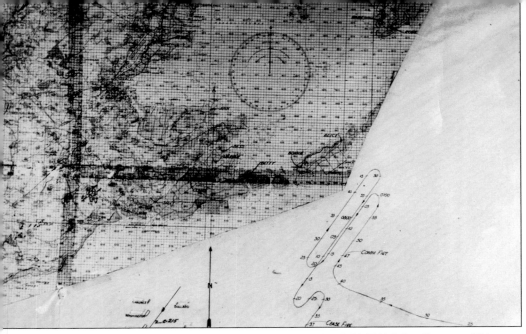

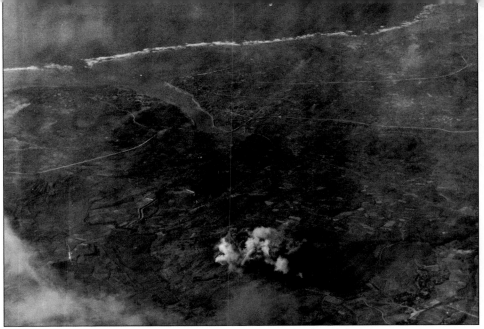

Following the 24 March naval bombardment and 1 April 1945 U.S. landings on Okinawa, USS *North Carolina* continued to serve off Okinawa. This chart shows the ship's bombardment track during a 19 April 1945 shelling of targets on the island. (Battleship *North Carolina*)

Toward the lower center, a concentration of 16-inch shells explodes on a target area a short distance inland on Okinawa. With a weight of around one ton and the advantage of high velocity, USS *North Carolina's* shells had a devastating effect. (Battleship *North Carolina*)

Ship Signal Flags

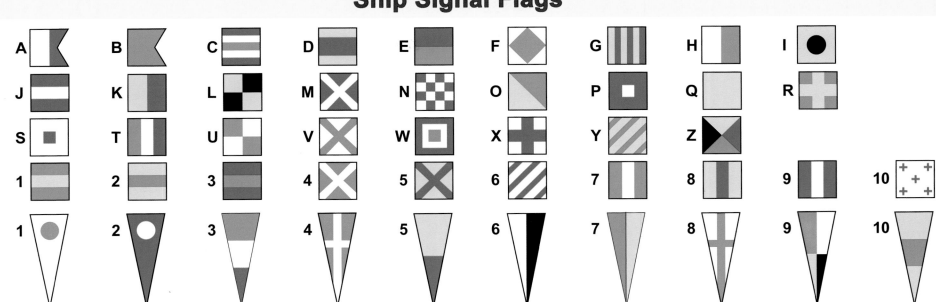

SHELL ENTERED HERE
(See Photo #1004-45)

5-11-45   2003-45
IT AFT AT DAMAGED PORT MK 37, MOD. 3, #2 DIR
& FDN. COLUMN AT FR 100

On 8 April 1945, during an intensive kamikaze attack on the U.S. fleet off Okinawa, the *North Carolina* suffered a "friendly fire" accident when a 5-inch common projectile struck the foundation of Sky Two, the port secondary-battery director, killing three crewmen and wounding 44. The projectile's entry hole is to the rear of the man kneeling on the scaffolding around the director's foundation. After the projectile struck the structure, the director was out of commission until repairs could be performed. (Battleship *North Carolina*)

An 11 May 1945 photo shows the external repairs to the area where the 5-inch projectile punctured the foundation of Sky Two, the port amidships Mk. 37 Mod. 3 secondary battery director on 8 April. The arrow points to the patch over the hole, a circular piece of steel. Crumpling is still visible on the top of the foundation. The repairs, performed at Pearl Harbor, also included restoring the director to operating condition. In the foreground is one of the ship's 36-inch searchlights, with the lens on the front swung open. (Battleship *North Carolina*)

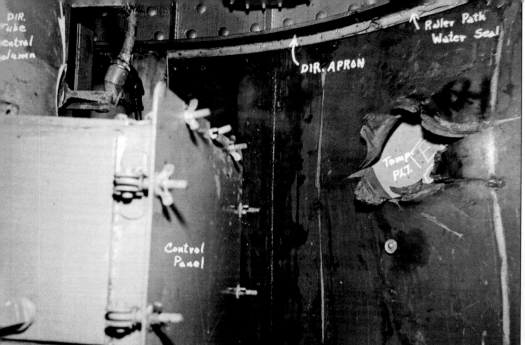

An 11 May 1945 view from inside Sky Two shows the interior of the entry hole punched through the Mk. 37 Mod. 3 secondary-battery director by the 5-inch projectile. The temporary repairs performed at sea made no effort to trim off the shards around the entry hole. However, the permanent repairs made at Pearl Harbor immediately after this photo was taken were much more complete. (Battleship *North Carolina*)

North Carolina crewmen gather solemnly on deck to witness the burial at sea of Edward E. Brenn, Carl E. Karams, and John M. Watson on 7 April 1945. All three had been killed in the friendly-fire incident the previous day. Each body was placed in a canvas shroud weighted with two 5-inch projectiles. The fourth man killed 6 April 1945, Eldon Means, was lost at sea when the Kingfisher he crewed capsized. (Battleship *North Carolina*)

Camouflage Measure 22 was applied to *North Carolina* in late 1945 and remained on the ship until she was drydocked for inactivation in June 1947. Prior to VJ day, the decks were camouflaged with a coat of 20-B Deck Blue paint, but the crew holystoned the decks back to bare teak during the return trip to the East Coast after the end of the war.

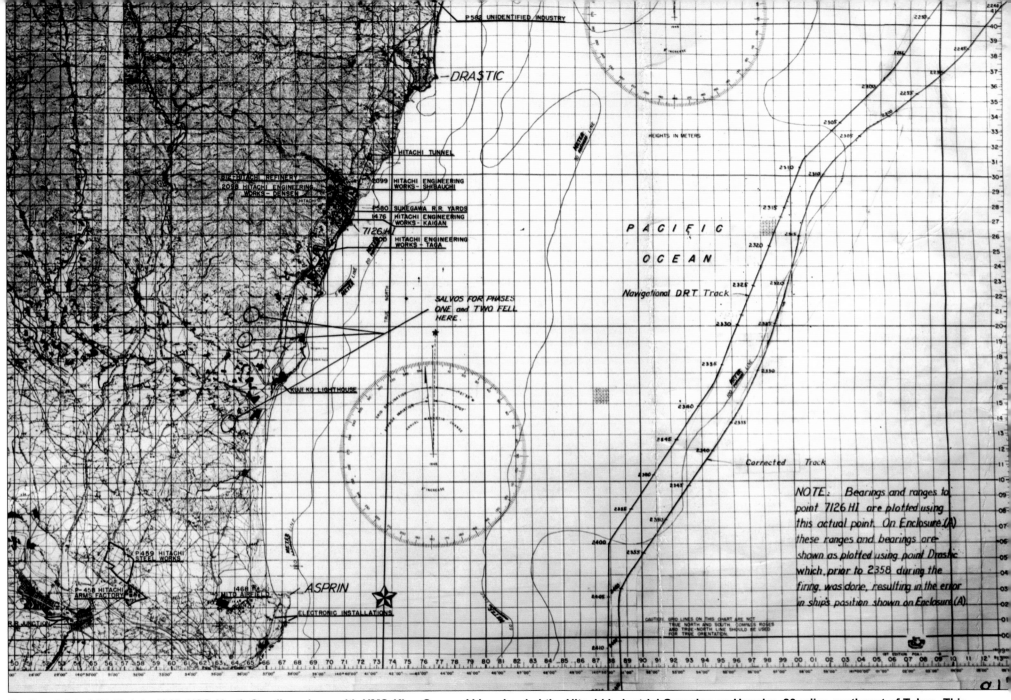

On the night of 17-18 July 1945, USS *North Carolina,* along with HMS *King George V,* bombarded the Hitachi Industrial Complex on Honshu, 80 miles northeast of Tokyo. This chart shows the bombardment track of the *North Carolina* during that mission. (Battleship *North Carolina*)

During a transit of the Panama Canal on 11 October 1945, the USS *North Carolina* passes through a lock. With the war concluded, camouflage paint was no longer necessary on the teak of the decks, so the crew had holystoned the Deck Blue paint off the teak. Deck Blue remained on the gun house roofs. Vought OS2U Kingfishers are mounted on the catapults. (Battleship *North Carolina*)

As these sailors on the USS *North Carolina* could affirm, as long as there is a United States Navy with ships with wooden decks, there will be holystoning. This venerable naval ritual originally involved rubbing the decks with holystone to brighten the decks, but these sailors are doing it with sand and wooden blocks on push-handles. (Battleship *North Carolina*)

The USS *North Carolina* transits the Panama Canal on 11 October 1945, having just departed from the locks in the background. In the ship's Measure 22 camouflage, the demarcation is evident between the Navy Blue below the lowest part of the sheer on the hull and the Haze Gray on vertical surfaces above that point. (Battleship *North Carolina*)

After the war, the *North Carolina* was overhauled at the New York Naval Shipyard at Brooklyn and is shown at that base in May 1946. The ship was still painted in Measure 22 camouflage. The ship's number, 55, had been painted on the side of the hull toward the stern and aft of the hawse pipe for the anchor. Signal flags are flying from the halyards. (National Archives)

Photographed from off the bow at the New York Naval Shipyard on 25 May 1946, the *North Carolina* displays the demarcation between the Navy Blue below the lowest point of the sheer of the hull and the Haze Gray above it. The number 55 is faintly visible aft of the port hawse pipe. The port anchor is exposed, displaying details of its shank and flukes. (National Archives)

The stern of the *North Carolina* is emphasized in this view taken at New York Naval Shipyard on 25 May 1946, with a tugboat operating to the port side. The ship's name is picked out in light-colored paint over the Navy Blue paint on the stern. The ship's number, 55, is painted on each side of the hull, just forward of the 40mm gun tubs on the fantail. (National Archives)

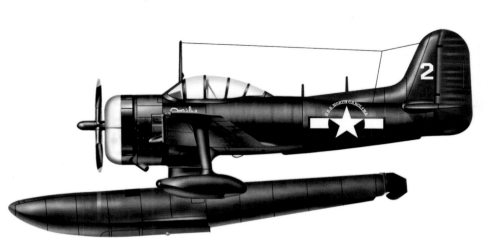

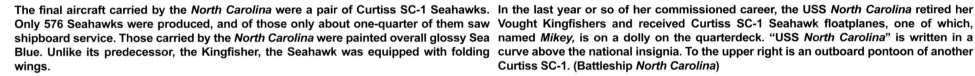

The final aircraft carried by the *North Carolina* were a pair of Curtiss SC-1 Seahawks. Only 576 Seahawks were produced, and of those only about one-quarter of them saw shipboard service. Those carried by the *North Carolina* were painted overall glossy Sea Blue. Unlike its predecessor, the Kingfisher, the Seahawk was equipped with folding wings.

Queenie was another Curtiss SC-1 Seahawk assigned to the *North Carolina*. It exhibits a checkerboard paint scheme on the cowl. The Curtiss SC was a single-seat scout floatplane that first entered the service with the U.S. Navy in late October 1944 but did not see active operations until June 1945. It was designed to be able to hold its own in a dogfight if necessary. (Battleship *North Carolina*)

In the last year or so of her commissioned career, the USS *North Carolina* retired her Vought Kingfishers and received Curtiss SC-1 Seahawk floatplanes, one of which, named *Mikey,* is on a dolly on the quarterdeck. "USS *North Carolina*" is written in a curve above the national insignia. To the upper right is an outboard pontoon of another Curtiss SC-1. (Battleship *North Carolina*)

Queenie comes astern of the USS *North Carolina,* as the crane hoist cable is being readied to bring the plane back aboard. The pilot, standing in the cockpit, will catch the cable and attach it to the plane. In the twin-seat Kingfishers previously assigned to the *North Carolina,* the radioman/observer in the rear seat had been tasked with grappling the hoist cable. (Battleship *North Carolina*)

A Curtiss SC-1 Seahawk is being hoisted aboard the USS *North Carolina,* the pilot still sitting in the cockpit. A dolly toward the right awaits placement under the center pontoon of the floatplane. The starboard catapult of the *North Carolina* had been removed by this point, but the catapult foundation remained in place, visible to the far left of the photograph. (Battleship *North Carolina*)

Two sailors standing on a mushroom ventilator in the aft port 20mm antiaircraft battery watch *Queenie* during a launch. A powder charge equivalent to that of a 5-inch shell has shot the launch cart, bearing the center pontoon of the Seahawk. Hydraulic bumpers on top of the end of the catapult will absorb the shock of the launch cart when it reaches the end of its travel. (Battleship *North Carolina*)

Sailors line up to go below decks in this scene showing a Curtiss SC-1 Seahawk resting on the port catapult of USS *North Carolina.* Temporary diagonal stays are attached to the center pontoon and the outboard pontoon struts. The cowl has a checkerboard scheme. To the left is turret three, with its starboard rangefinder housing jutting prominently. Stacked atop the gun house are life rafts. To the right of center, a sailor is leaning his right hand on an object with a dark-colored cover over it. This was a warping winch, and there was also one on the opposite side of turret three. Warping winches were used, in conjunction with hawsers fastened to a dock, to move the ship into place along the dock. (Battleship *North Carolina*)

The USS *North Carolina* is underway at sea during June 1946. The starboard catapult is absent. She is still wearing her final World War II camouflage scheme, Measure 22, not yet having been painted in her final scheme before being decommissioned, overall Haze Gray (5-H). Her teak decks are particularly resplendent. (Battleship *North Carolina*)

During the summer of 1946, the *North Carolina* would visit Annapolis, Maryland, to take aboard two separate groups of U.S. Naval Academy midshipmen for training cruises. However, in the new postwar order, with no immediate wars on the horizon and where navies could be wiped out in concentrated nuclear attacks, battleships such as the *North Carolina* were increasingly seen as redundant and obsolescent. (Battleship *North Carolina*)

The *North Carolina* steams through placid waters in a photo taken from an altitude of 300 feet on 3 June 1946. The bare teak on the main deck has a light color. The forecastle deck, the anchor plates (or chafing plates), and other metal fixtures on the main deck retain the Deck Blue color that was part of the Measure 22 camouflage system. The absence of the starboard catapult is clearly visible; crewmen are lounging on top of the foundation for that catapult. (Battleship *North Carolina*)

Inactivation

Her post-war activities as a training ship concluded, *North Carolina* entered drydock at the New York Naval Shipyard, Brooklyn, New York, on 16 May 1947 for underwater inactivation work and preservation commensurate with her being assigned to the Reserve Fleet. The interior of the ship was sealed, divided into seven zones and dehumidification equipment installed. Lightweight "igloos" were placed over the remaining 40mm gun mounts and desiccants added to slow deterioration. Her search radar antenna was removed and stowed. The exterior of the ship was painted overall 5-H Haze Gray, a color scheme she would wear for the next several decades. The deactivation work at the shipyard was completed on 19 June 1947.

She was decommissioned and placed in "Inactive Status" as a vessel "Out of Commission in Reserve" on 27 June 1947 and was laid up as part of the Reserve Fleet in Bayonne, New Jersey, across the harbor from where she had been built. She would be tied abreast of her solitary sister ship, USS *Washington,* and would remain there for 15 years. During that time periodic maintenance and occasional modifications would be performed. Between 1950 and 1953 both catapults were removed, as well as the booms from both boat cranes. Over time the main and secondary fire control radar arrays were also removed.

The port side of the USS *North Carolina* is viewed from the floor of Drydock No. 5 in 1947, providing a good sense of the monolithic presence of the hull. The battleship's number, 55, is painted aft of the port hawse pipe. The absence of the SK 2 air-search antenna on top of the foremast is very clear in this view. The main mast is also visible. (Battleship *North Carolina*)

This view of the *North Carolina* in Drydock No. 5 at the New York Navy Yard is thought to date from early 1947. The men walking on the floor of the drydock provide a sense of the huge scale of the ship. A good view is provided of the bulbous bow. Draft marks are visible on both sides of the bow. The *North Carolina* is still in Measure 22 camouflage. The belt armor is clearly visible above and below the waterline aft of the bow. Radar antennas are still present on top of the Mk. 37 and Mk. 38 directors, but the SK 2 air-search antenna has been removed from the foremast. Radio antennas and rigging are still present. (Battleship *North Carolina*)

Another photo of USS *North Carolina* in Drydock No. 5 shows the aspect of the ship from the starboard side. On the foredeck aft of the jackstaff, the splinter shields for the forward 20mm antiaircraft batteries are in view. Several of these drydock photos indicate that the rims of the bullnoses at the forecastle were painted a darker color than the surrounding Haze Gray. (Battleship *North Carolina*)

The U.S. flag waving smartly from the USS *North Carolina* is viewed from astern during her time in Drydock No. 5. Demarcations are visible on the 40mm gun tubs on the fantail between the lower color, Navy Blue, and the upper color, Haze Gray. Sections of scaffolding have been moved up close to the hull to enable workmen to perform maintenance and repairs. (Battleship *North Carolina*)

Fifteen months after decommissioning, the *North Carolina* rests at the New York Navy Yard on 25 September 1948. The ship has been "mothballed" – placed into a state of preservation – prior moving to Bayonne, New Jersey, to join other Reserve Fleet vessels: deactivated warships that could be restored to active service in time of war. Interestingly, while the starboard catapult had previously been ordered removed, such a catapult was subsequently ordered reinstalled, and is visible here. (Battleship *North Carolina*)

Ultimately, many of *North Carolina's* smaller components, both internal and external, including parts of some of the 40mm mounts, were salvaged for use on active Navy warships. Then in 1960, *North Carolina* was finally deemed obsolete and declared surplus, and she was slated for scrapping.

Word of the veteran fighting ship's impending demise reached James S. Craig, Jr., a businessman in Wilmington. Craig immediately launched a campaign to save the famed Showboat, contacting Governor Luther Hodges as well as incoming Governor Terry Sanford, a WWII paratrooper. Governor Hodges asked the Navy to delay the disposal of the ship and work began to find a new life for the *North Carolina,* with fellow Wilmington businessman, Hugh Morton, joining Craig in the effort. Their campaign quickly captured the attention of Wilmington's leading political and commercial circles, and soon the campaigners tapped Cyril Adams, a Houston-based marine engineer who had been involved in the successful effort to save the Battleship *Texas.* Adams recommended a berthing point in Wilmington, where the ship would be relatively safe from hurricanes.

The citizens of North Carolina rallied to save the legendary battleship named for their state. Everyone from school children to prominent citizens and businesses donated to preserve her, and *North Carolina* was ultimately saved from the scrapper's torch (a fate which befell her sister). After a tow to her new home in Wilmington, North Carolina, she was pushed into a specially-dredged berth and since 28 April 1962 has served as both a war memorial and a museum, hosting over 10 million visitors.

Ships of the Reserve Fleet are moored at the Bayonne Naval Supply Depot on the New Jersey side of New York Harbor on 15 April 1953. The two ships in the second row from the right are the *North Carolina* (dockside) and the *Washington.* Also in storage was an assortment of cruisers, fleet carriers, escort carriers, and support ships. (Battleship *North Carolina*)

On 2 February 1950 the *North Carolina* (the second ship on the right) and her sister ship, the *Washington,* were photographed in "mothballs" at the Bayonne Naval Supply Depot. Measures implemented to preserve the *North Carolina* during what could be an extended period of storage included covers fitted over the wildcats, which actuated the raising and lowering of the anchors. (Battleship *North Carolina*)

A view of the *North Carolina* (right) and the *Washington* while stored at the Bayonne Naval Supply Depot illustrates some details on the *North Carolina* that were absent on the *Washington,* such as the protruding structure above the front center of the pilot house, and Stryker's Bridge, midway up the forward fire-control tower, installed at Pearl Harbor in 1943. (Battleship *North Carolina*)

129

During her time in mothballs at Bayonne, the *North Carolina's* exterior paint deteriorated; many areas of peeling and rust are apparent in this view from the port aft quarter. Covers had been installed over the gun openings on the 5-inch mounts and 16-inch turrets to keep out the elements. Dome-shaped igloos were secured over the 40mm gun mounts to preserve them. (Battleship *North Carolina*)

Sitting in storage for long periods without maintenance is not good for any ship. Peeling paint and corrosion are widespread on all surfaces of the *North Carolina* in this view of the port amidships area, at Bayonne. Prior to being placed in mothballs, the ship's rigging, radio and radar antennas, 20mm antiaircraft guns, and removable equipment such as life rafts and boats were removed. (Battleship *North Carolina*)

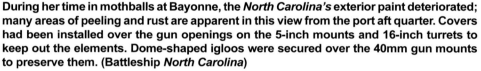

This view of the *North Carolina* (foreground) and her sister ship the *Washington* allows a comparative view of their forward upper superstructures and forward fire-control towers. Gone from the foremast is the SK 2 air-search radar antenna, and the SG surface-search radar antennas have been removed from the foremast and main mast. The jackstaff on the forecastle is lowered. (Battleship *North Carolina*)

The *North Carolina* is moored to the dock at the Bayonne Naval Supply Depot in August 1961. The following month the ship would begin its voyage south to its new home in Wilmington, North Carolina. The rust and peeling paint visible on the hull in the preceding photo appears to have been chipped off in this photo, and touchups with a different shade of paint have been made. (University of North Carolina)

After 15 years in mothballs, the *North Carolina* was slated for scrapping when a citizens' group purchased the ship for $330,000 for a war memorial to be located in Wilmington. In this dockside ceremony at Bayonne in June 1961, the ship was transferred from the Navy to the people of North Carolina. The stern of the battleship *New Jersey* is to the left, and the *North Carolina* is to the right. (Battleship *North Carolina*)

Following a transit from Bayonne, New Jersey, south, the *North Carolina* proceeds under tow up the Cape Fear River on 1 October 1961, on the last leg of the trip to Wilmington. Splotchy touchup paint patterns are visible on the ship, particularly on the side of the hull. Although this measure of maintenance had been performed on the ship, it would need much more preservation work. (Battleship *North Carolina*)

Preparations are underway to tow the battleship *North Carolina* from Bayonne to her new home in Wilmington, North Carolina. Several tugboats accomplished this task. Here, a chain has been rigged through the ship's port hawse pipe, while a line that has been shot to bring aboard a tow line passes through the starboard hawse pipe. (Battleship *North Carolina*)

On 1 October 1961, tugboats maneuver the *North Carolina* up the Cape Fear River past downtown Wilmington on the far shore, with the U.S. Customs House to the right. The channel where the battleship would make her new home is just out of the view to the left. In the preceding days, after reaching the mouth of the Cape Fear River, the ship had lowered its starboard anchor to ride out a storm. Since the ship had no steam to power the windlass to raise the anchor, it was necessary to cut the anchor chain before proceeding. Later, the Coast Guard salvaged the anchor, which is now on display at the ship. (Battleship *North Carolina*)

Tugboats nudge the *North Carolina* toward the channel at the bottom right where it will permanently rest at anchor, on 1 October 1961. The white boat moored along the Wilmington waterfront was *Fergus's Ark,* a floating restaurant that was formerly the *General Frederick C. Hodgkins.* Shortly, the *Ark* would have a very close call with the *North Carolina.* (Battleship *North Carolina*)

As photographed from a Wilmington rooftop, as the tugboats were easing the *North Carolina* into her channel opposite downtown Wilmington, things got out of control, and the stern of the battleship grazed *Fergus's Ark* (bottom of photo). The dome-shaped "igloos" had protected the 40mm gun mounts from the elements while the ship was in mothballs. (Battleship *North Carolina*)

A photographer captured this close-up view of the *North Carolina's* collision with the *Ark.* The beleaguered restaurant boat is toward the left, with the *North Carolina's* stern pressing against its side. To the right, tugboats work frantically to move the battleship forward. The owner of *Fergus's Ark* sued the *North Carolina* Battleship Memorial Commission for $25,000 in damages. (Battleship *North Carolina*)

Safely extricated from its brush with the *Ark,* the *North Carolina* is being coaxed into her anchorage channel to the right by tugboats. In addition to the igloos, other signs of the ship's tenure in mothballs include covers over many of the portholes in the superstructure, covers over the gun openings in the 5-inch and 16-inch gun mounts, and covers over the tops of the funnels. (Battleship *North Carolina*)

The channel that the *North Carolina* would be berthed in was situated at a right angle to the Cape Fear River, and maneuvering the 728-foot-long battleship crosswise in a river that was 525 feet wide was an exacting, nerve-wracking process for the tugboat crews. It is evident from this and the preceding photos just how narrow the river and the entrance to the channel to the left were. (Battleship *North Carolina*)

Igloos are being removed from the 40mm gun tubs on the *North Carolina* at her slip at Wilmington. One of the igloos is being shuttled from the ship to the shore by means of a highline. In the foreground is an igloo, showing some details of its design, including the access door that was included so maintenance crews could enter the structure while the ship was in mothballs. (Battleship *North Carolina*)

The *North Carolina* is now in her berth, and the tugboats have begun to back away as crowds thronged on both banks watch the event unfold. Soon, the ship will be moored and preparations begun to ready her for her conversion into a memorial. Prominently absent is the starboard anchor, which was left on the bottom of the ocean off the entrance to the Cape Fear River. It has since been recovered by the Coast Guard and is now displayed on the foredeck of the ship. (Battleship *North Carolina*)

On 28 April 1962, the dedication ceremony for the USS *North Carolina* Battleship Memorial was held on the quarterdeck of the battleship in her permanent slip at Wilmington, North Carolina. Dignitaries in attendance included retired chief of naval operations, Admiral Arleigh Burke and North Carolina Governor Terry Sanford. (Battleship *North Carolina*)

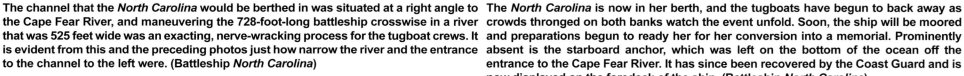

For some time, the battleship *North Carolina* was painted gray overall, with large, white ship's numbers, shadowed with black, painted on each side of the bow, in the style of U.S. Navy ships in the postwar years. (Department of Defense)

As viewed from off the port stern, a Vought OS2U Kingfisher is displayed on the fantail of the *North Carolina.* The horizontal object casting the shadow on the side of the hull forward of the aft 40mm gun tub is a boat boom. (Department of Defense)

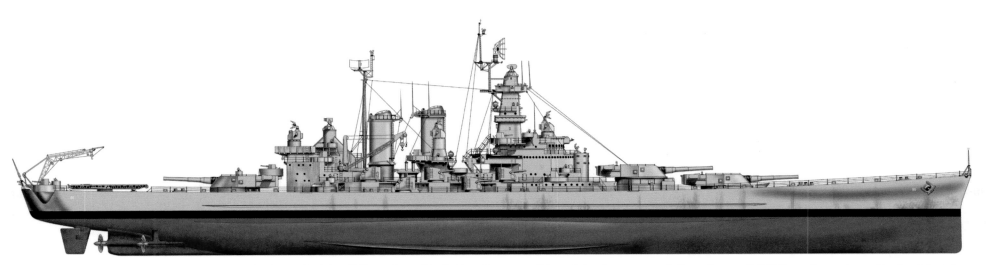

From her June 1947 inactivation and through the end of the 20th century, *North Carolina* wore this paint scheme, consisting of overall 5-H Haze Gray above the boot topping. Wooden decks were holystoned natural teak.

Following an illustrious career in World War II and years of neglect in mothballs with the Reserve Fleet, the USS *North Carolina* enjoys a well-deserved place of honor in Wilmington, North Carolina, serving as a memorial to the men and women of that state who served and died in the U.S. armed forces during World War II. The ship is open to the public, who can walk the decks and explore many of the spaces within the turrets, gun mounts, superstructure, and below decks, and experience the feel, look, and scents of a U.S. fast battleship of World War II. (Battleship *North Carolina*)